PREPARING FOR THE NEXT CORRECTION

THE 2018 MARKET BUBBLE SURVIVAL GUIDE

J. Kevin Meaders, J.D., CFP®, ChFC, CLU

J. Kevin Meaders/Magellan Planning Group, Inc.
4170 Ashford Dunwoody Rd
Suite 480
Atlanta, GA 30319

www.magellanplanning.com
kevin@magellanplanning.com

Cover design by Platinum Advisor Strategies

Printed by CreateSpace, An Amazon.com Company
Available on Kindle

The Market Bubble Survival Guide/J. Kevin Meaders – First Edition

ISBN:1732157022
ISBN-13: 978-1732157026

DISCLAIMER

Nothing herein should be taken as specific investment advice. I have no idea about your current holdings, your risk tolerance, your future goals, your wants or needs, or anything else. All I am doing here is telling you what we are doing, and have done, for our clients in general.

I am giving you my rationale for why we have taken and plan to take these actions, but you have to decide what is right for you. There is no substitute to sitting down face-to-face with a holistic fee-based Certified Financial Planner Professional who can properly analyze your specific situation.

If you do not have an advisor you are comfortable with, and you agree with the steps I outline in this book, I encourage you to contact me. My company, Magellan Planning Group, Inc., is selectively accepting new clients nationwide.

TABLE OF CONTENTS

PREFACE

Anyone who was invested in stocks in 2008 experienced a loss of at least a third of their portfolio—for some, even more. What if I told you another 2008-type event could be on the horizon? And what if I told you that there might be a way to explain—even track and predict—these huge stock market crashes? Well, there is.

Few people have really studied economics from a hands-on perspective. Most economists are just Ph.D. theorists who really have no experience managing money.

As a hands-on money manager, I could not accept the industry standard that market crashes are natural occurrences and must be endured as part of the investment process. As I looked around for a logical explanation, I encountered the Austrian School of Economics, another group of Ph.D. theorists, but with explanations that seemed to correlate exactly with what I was seeing first hand.

Eventually, through enough immersion into the Ph.D.'s world of economic theory, particularly the Austrian School, I was able to discern key elements from which I derived a useful hands-on approach to managing money. This has worked well for our clients during both the dot.com bust in 2000 and the 2008 Great Recession.

I have tried to put my methods into easy-to-understand terms and keep it short, so as to help as many investors as possible survive in the coming market bubble collapse.

Finally, economics is no longer esoteric and nebulous, but useful in a real-world way to anyone who reads this book.

I

PUTTING IT ALL INTO PERSPECTIVE

The unfortunate truth is this: Most investors react irrationally.[1] They are people, and people become emotionally tied to their money. It is almost impossible to divorce emotion from investing. Everyone knows it. And even knowing this, most analysts still apply rules and formulae that require a very important premise: that the subject will act as a rational person would. A patent fallacy.

How beneficial is it to rely on archaic valuations and expectations when the current subject of these no longer fits into the definitions for which the formulae were developed in the first place? Imagine the quintessential investor in 1985. Was he (and yes, it was mostly men) using the internet to move money around in his 401k plan during the middle of the night while watching events unfold around the world instantaneously on CNN?

No, the world turned at a much slower pace. Your news was limited to the morning paper, and then a synopsis of those repeated headlines on the 6 o'clock evening news. Your choices included CBS, NBC, and ABC. And for the radical intelligentsia, there was PBS NewsHour with Jim Lehrer. Other than some periodicals, that was the limit of your daily information on the world around you. Sometimes international developments could take days or even weeks to make it to mainstream media, and often, it never made it at all.

---

1 *Reading Between the Lines of Investor Biases*, Journal of Financial Planning, January 2005.

To young people who can't remember a time before the internet, the idea of this must be mind-boggling.

No, the typical investor before the 1990's had to pick up the phone and call someone—yes, a broker. This broker had information on investments that he would divulge to his client, and oftentimes there was a conversation about the most prudent path to take. Surely there was bad advice, and undoubtedly there were unfortunate decisions, but the pace of it all was much slower and limited to banker's hours. There were far fewer investors and the information was much more limited. The point here is that—before the internet—investors rarely made decisions on their own, without at least a conversation and some pointed research, usually in the form of a prospectus, or a "red herring", a sort of unofficial pre-prospectus.

Indeed, the comparison with today could not be starker. Millennials sit around in the middle of the night plugged into Twitter and Facebook placing instantaneous buys and sells on their internet-based platform, sometimes even on their smart phone. Often these decisions are based on rumors or hunches—rarely, if ever, do they read the prospectus. The *pro*spectus has become a *retro*spectus, used mostly by lawyers after something has gone awry. These Millennials weren't in the market in 2008, or 2000, or 1987. And like all prior generations, they are in for a rude awakening.

But for you, who are reading this now, you remember some of those times, and you are experienced or wise enough to know that our current bull market can't last forever—it never does. So, when the next bubble bursts, be ready. Have a plan, and calmly see it through. Remember, panic is your worst enemy. It leads to irrational decisions—sometimes decisions that are irreparable.

II

IS THERE REALLY A BUBBLE?

This is where things are going to start sounding a little weird—perhaps some things you've never heard before. It's also going to sound a little esoteric and unfamiliar, but I would argue this is not by accident. You may wonder what all of this has to do with *you*, but hang in there, and it will all become clear in due course.

The first thing you need to realize about our stock markets—and I would argue all markets—is that things happen in cycles. Sometimes these cycles are natural, like good harvest seasons and poor ones. Others, like fluctuations in the Fed Funds Rate, are man-made. To truly understand the modern boom/bust cycle, one must understand the Federal Reserve System, the Mandrake Mechanism (monetary expansion through credit), and the history of fiat currencies.

John Maynard Keynes. You've heard the name. Was it Econ 101 in college? Isn't he associated with economics somehow? Keynesian Economics. Where have I heard that? Well, no matter what you know of Keynes or don't know, he, more than any other person, affects your life in everyday ways. He affects your job, your investments, your savings, your pensions, your retirement benefits, your taxes, and your entire financial security—right down to the value of the pennies in your pocket. Considering all this, it might be prudent to learn a little more about Keynes, don't you think?

Keynesian Economics was borne out of the Industrial Revolution as a sort of defining relationship between industrialists and labor (yes, our story goes back that far). The industrialist's motive was to maximize profitability by paying the lowest possible wage. According to Keynes, as a result of the refusal of workers to accept a lower wage, unemployment ensues. Thus, unemployment is the direct result of the workers' refusal to accept a lower wage. Keynes writes:

> A classical economist may sympathize with labour in refusing to accept a cut in its money wage…; but scientific integrity forces him to declare that this refusal is, nevertheless, at the bottom of the trouble.[2]

So Keynes postulates another way to reduce the worker's wage: not by reducing the number of dollars the worker receives, but by reducing the amount of "stuff" that each of his dollars will buy. The number of dollars the worker actually receives Keynes calls "money wage," but the amount of goods and services purchased for a dollar is the "real wage."

It would not do you much good to earn $1 million per year if every trip to the grocery store cost you $50,000. In real terms, the worker who earns $100 per year is wealthier if an identical trip to the grocery store cost only $1. The nominal amount—the money wage—is meaningless. The power to purchase—the real wage—is everything.

The answer, therefore, according to Keynes, is not a cut in money wages since workers would resist, but a cut in real wages, which is simply a loss in purchasing power due to a rise in the cost of living. If you reduce a worker's money wage, he earns less money per hour. If you reduce his real wage, the money that he earns will buy him less because prices are higher. Keynes further explains that:

> Since there is, as a rule, no means of securing a simultaneous and equal reduction of money wages in all industries, it is in the interest of all workers to resist a reduction in their own particular case. In fact, a movement by employers to revise money wage

---

[2] *The General Theory of Employment, Interest and Money*. John Maynard Keynes, 1935, pg 16

> bargains downward will be much more strongly resisted than a gradual and automatic lowering of real wages as a result of rising prices.[3]

There you have it from the man himself. It is much easier to reduce the real wage through inflation and loss of purchasing power than to reduce the money wage because…

> …it would be impracticable to resist every reduction of real wages, due to a change in the purchasing power of money which affects all workers alike; and in fact, reductions of real wages arising in this way are not, as a rule, resisted unless they proceed to an extreme degree… Every trade union will put up some resistance to a cut in money wages, however small. But since no trade union would dream of striking on every occasion of a rise in the cost of living, they do not raise the obstacle…**Thus it is fortunate that the workers, though unconsciously…do not resist reductions of real wages…**[4]

Meaning they don't resist rising prices—inflation. Perhaps one could argue his doctrine of intentional inflation was directed to the industrialists alone. One can imagine thousands of workers toiling away in the company factory, living on company land, renting a company flat, and buying all of their essentials from the company store. In this way the industrialists might control the real wage—the cost of living—as well as the money wage.

But Keynes is speaking to the powers that be: the "governing and academic classes of this generation."[5] And grateful governments latched on quickly and firmly. Finally, they had an academic who defended—nay, promoted—the intentional depreciation of purchasing power through inflation. And that means war!

---

[3] *The General Theory of Employment, Interest and Money*. John Maynard Keynes, 1935 pg 223

[4] Ibid. pgs 14,15

[5] *The General Theory of Employment, Interest and Money*. John Maynard Keynes, 1935

See, there is an age-old saying: "To carry on a successful war, three things are needed: money, money, and yet more money."[6] When governments go to war they have almost unlimited conscripts, but not an unlimited supply of money. To get the required money, a government has only three options:

1. Borrow it from other countries and the population through the sale of bonds.
2. Raise taxes and tariffs and reduce benefits.
3. Create money and force everyone to accept it through legal tender laws.

In the United States, we utilize all three, but two of them have limits. One can only borrow what others are willing (and able) to loan, and large increases in taxes are politically unpopular. Thus, the remaining choice of money creation is the clear favorite, and as renowned economist Hans F. Sennholz eloquently points out in his 1979 book, *Age of Inflation,* the trend is worrisome at best:

> In the past, the inflations were of relatively short durations, limited to periods of national emergency when the central government was called upon to finance extraordinary defense expenditures. After the end of hostilities monetary stability soon returned as the emergency financing was abandoned. Today, public demand for governmental services never abates, in wartime and in peacetime, but seems to accelerate year after year. In fact, the more government spends on economic and social objectives the louder the public clamor for more services seems to become. Thus, the temporary emergencies that in the past gave occasion for extraordinary defense expenditures and inflationary financing have given way to a permanent emergency of social service and inflationary financing. It is true that inflation can never be permanent, for it must come to

[6] Gian Giacome Trivulzio, w*hen Louis XII asked him what was needed in order to conduct war.*

> an end with the total destruction of the currency.[7]

This was written in 1979, but it sounds like it was written yesterday. Obviously, the "total destruction" has not yet occurred, though from my perspective it sure seems imminent. And yet, it probably seemed imminent to Professor Sennholz when he wrote that almost four decades ago.

Nevertheless, what Keynes and his followers have always refused to admit is that every period of monetary expansion is followed by a period of painful correction. Indeed, the initial flood of new, cheap money creates a boom—a tide that raises all boats, but in due course a crash inevitably ensues. As anti-Keynesian Economics Professor Ludwig von Mises explains:

> The wavelike movement affecting the economic system, the recurrence of periods of boom which are followed by periods of depression, is the unavoidable outcome of the attempts, repeated again and again, to lower the gross market rate of interest by means of credit expansion. There is no means of avoiding the final collapse of a boom brought about by credit expansion. The alternative is only whether the crisis should come sooner as the result of voluntary abandonment of the further credit expansion, or later as a final and total catastrophe of the currency system involved.[8]

---

[7] *Age of Inflation.* Hans F. Sennholz, 1979, pg 62

[8] *Human Action: A Treatise on Economics.* Ludwig von Mises, 1949, pg 570

III

VOODOO ECONOMICS

The total collapse of our currency system has not yet occurred because the more tenable alternative thus far has been the "abandonment of further credit expansion" though, indeed, as Mises foretold, recessions and depressions followed. To help illustrate Mises' point, take a close look at the chart of the Effective Fed Funds Rate on the following page. Note that the shaded areas indicate a recession—a bust. (In some cases, such as 1987, a bust may not fit the strict definition of "recession", so it is not shaded). Note that before every recession is the "abandonment" Mises spoke of, which I have labeled with a red "2". This is a raising of interest rates—an abandonment of easy credit.

Notice what happens just after almost every red 2: a bust, just as Mises says. And before the red 2 (which is a rise in rates), there is a lowering of rates which indicates the beginning of the "monetary expansion" (lower rates = cheap money), which I have likewise indicated with a green "**1**". Now take notice of what happens to the rates every time a recession occurs—more of the same—another artificial lowering of rates, creating yet again another boom-bust cycle.

Mises is right on. The Fed lowers rates to create a boom (1), a boom ensues. The Fed raises rates to control inflation (2), and then a bust strikes (recession), and then the Fed lowers rates again to create a boom (1). Every time, just like clockwork. Every green 1 is followed by a red 2 is followed by a recession (or bust) is followed by a green 1, *ad infinitum*.

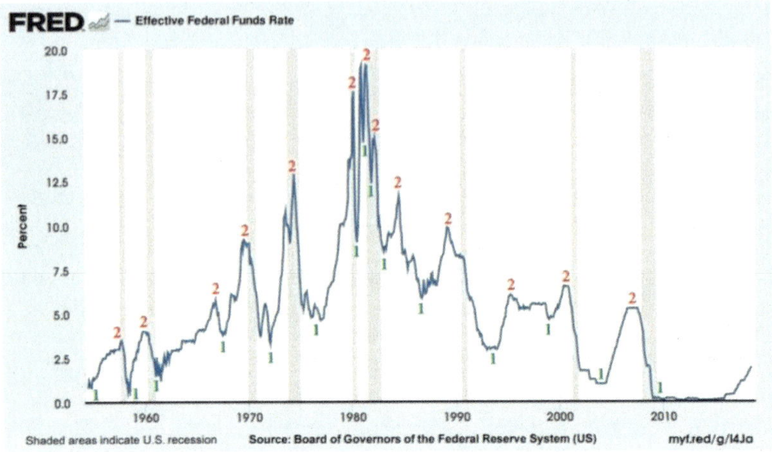

[9]

Finally, I want you to note the ever-increasing intensity of the monetary easing needed since 1980 (the downward trend of green 1s). Each time the Fed is forced to drive down rates because of the previous rate hike, the lower the rate has been.

Remember the late 1990's? The dot.com phenomenon was fully under way. The Munder Net-Net fund—remember that?—posted double digit returns for years in a row, sometimes triple digits. A lot of the growth during that time was real. The internet was real, and internet trading became the fashion, while internet stocks were the darlings of the market. The conduit became the commodity became the conduit, and entirely new industries grew out of garages.

This was when Alan Greenspan coined his famous "irrational exuberance" description of the market makers and internet investors. Prices were inflating, money was expanding, velocity was through the roof. And the Fed, worried about inflation, started raising rates, contracting the money supply, slowing velocity… and raising rates…raising rates… until, CRASH!

Now this is a big takeaway, because the lesson here is that

[9] FRED, Federal Reserve Bank of St. Louis; https://fred.stlouisfed.org/series/DFF (Set to Max)

the Fed never stops raising rates UNTIL the market crashes. That's how they know. It's the only way they know. Then, of course, once the market has tanked, it's time for stimulus again. Drop those rates, cut those jobs, cut that corporate spending, crank up that government spending, get those people in line for government benefits. Spend, spend, spend. Borrow, borrow, borrow. Print, print, print.

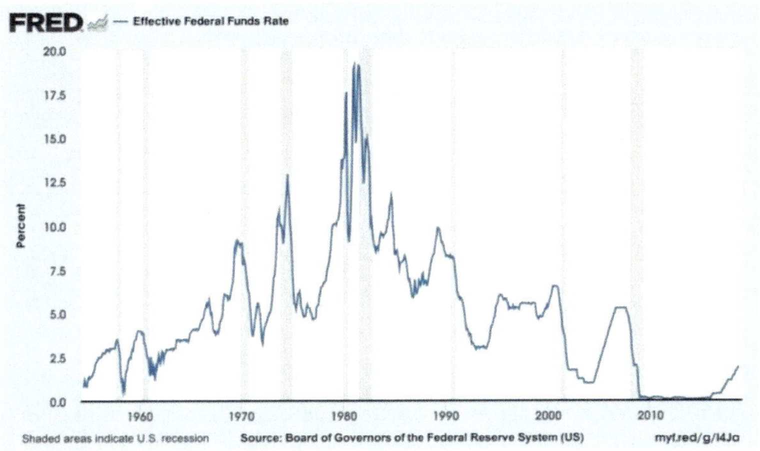

10

After the crash in 2008, the Fed reversed course and dropped rates down to as low as 98 basis points—a tad under 1%.

Perhaps you remember LIBOR at 1%?[11] It was the trend at the time to buy an adjustable rate mortgage (ARM) at 1%, nothing down, and no documentation. Generally, these loans could adjust after a period of 1-3 years, and they certainly did. True to their nature, the folks at the Fed started raising rates and mortgages started to adjust upwards. Then, they started to default.

Massive mortgage defaults caused banks to fail. Those that didn't fail sold off their inventories of high quality bonds to

[10] https://fred.stlouisfed.org/series/DFF (Set to Max)

[11] London Interbank Overnight Rate (LIBOR), which we now know was being illegally manipulated at that time.

stay afloat. The bond market crashed. AAA-rated insured municipal bonds were off by 35%—something that is NEVER supposed to happen. Even the bond insurers became insolvent; they were undercapitalized and over-leveraged.

Then the unthinkable happened: Lehman Brothers and Bear Sterns failed. The toxic debt was unwinding and taking all the players down with it. Then the Fed, along with the remaining big banks, convinced Congress to inject $700 billion with TARP (Troubled Asset Relief Program). This saved the remaining big banks from their own misdeeds.

The Fed injected massive amounts of artificial stimulus into the market by marking up the bank reserve balances at the Fed, hoping the banks would loan out money to everyone. But they didn't. And even if they had wanted to, no one was borrowing. They soon realized they could reinvest the short-term money that the Fed gave them into longer term bonds at the Fed, and arbitrage the difference in the interest rates, with absolutely zero risk. A great deal.

All this, of course, did nothing for the average person who was losing his home because he was foolish enough to "cash out" the equity in his house and reinvest in the booming stock market. For a while it worked—until interest rates climbed, his mortgage adjusted, and on top of that, his stocks crashed 40%. In many cases, he had to just walk away with ruined credit and ruined finances, and nowhere to live. Mortgage collapses and home repossessions hit an all-time high. But the big banks were safe, and profitable again, and *that* was the important thing to the bureaucrats.

TARP, QE, QE2, Operation Twist, QE3. Our monetary base went from just around $800 billion to a whopping $4 trillion. Stimulus, stimulus, stimulus

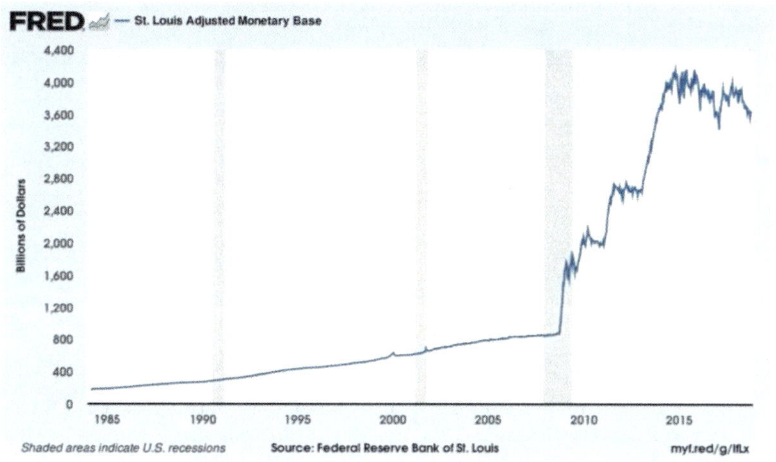

[12]

But the consumer was hit hard, and she wasn't buying, and she wasn't borrowing. The Dow Jones finally bottomed out around 6500![13] The auto industry was in trouble, and some James Taggart bureaucrat type had the great Keynesian stroke of genius to stimulate the auto industry—Cash for Clunkers—where perfectly good vehicles were required to be rendered utterly useless.

By January 2009, the Fed had dropped rates all the way down to 0.15%. That's 15% of 1%. By July of 2011, it was half of that, at 7 basis points. Very close to zero.

So here we are again, on another stock market tear that will surely end the way they always end. But when? And in any event what does one do about it? Is this not what you were just thinking?

Well, based on all that I just told you, at least you now have an edge. The first rule of surviving a mine field is the simple realization that you are in a mine field (!) and every step could be your last, so tread carefully. Knowing and understanding the boom-bust cycle is a real advantage that we can use to both

[12] https://fred.stlouisfed.org/series/BASE (Set to Max)

[13] The Dow closed at 6547 on Monday, March 9, 2009. As of this writing, it is over 24,000.

make money in the boom, but more importantly protect ourselves during the bust. We know a boom has come and is here. We know we are in a bubble, and we know that a bust will inevitably follow. What we don't know is quite when. Nor do we know the eventual size of the bubble prior to the burst.

Nonetheless, we know what to look for and what to expect—eventually—so we can position ourselves accordingly. I call these man-made economic booms and accompanying busts, "Fed Super-Cycles." The key deter-mination is whether—and to what degree—monetary supply is contracting or expanding.

Unfortunately, one of the key determining factors—the degree—at which monetary supply is contracting or expanding, is not readily discoverable, mainly because there are so many variables at work. There are these man-made forces of raising or lowering interest rates, of raising and lowering bank reserve requirements, and of expanding or contracting the money supply, but there are other natural forces at work, too. These other forces include the pervasive economic milieu of supply and demand, the natural tendency of price anomalies created by artificial manipulation to equalize, and my personal favorite, the inescapable law of unintended consequences.

Fortunately, though it is impossible to know the exact degree at which the money supply is expanding or contracting at any given time, it is at least possible to easily figure out in which direction we are headed. Are we expanding (lowering rates, stable or lower bank reserve ratios, expanding the balance sheet), or are we contracting (climbing rates, stable or higher bank reserve ratios, reducing the balance sheet)?

IV

WAYS OUR ECONOMY IS MANIPULATED

You've now seen how the Fed has historically artificially raised and lowered interest rates and you've now seen how the Fed has increased our Monetary Base from around $850 Billion to over $4 Trillion. But few people (and almost no one in Congress) understand how these financial schemes actually work, and least of all the real and sometimes disastrous effects they can have on the economy.

Essentially, there are three ways that our economy is manipulated by the Federal Reserve. The first and most obvious is the ability to raise and lower the base interest rate that is at the heart of all the other interest rates. The second way is through expanding or contracting the money supply by expanding or contracting the Fed's Balance Sheet. And the third is to regulate how many dollars must be held in reserve by banks for every $100 they loan out. Let's look at each of these in turn.

THE IMPORTANCE OF INTEREST RATES

It may not seem like a big deal, but interest rates can have the most significant effects on our economy. Interest rates represent the price of money. Think about that for a minute. Essentially when you borrow money, you are renting it. The interest that you pay is the price of renting that money for the period you are using it. Like anything else, when the price is low more people are willing to buy it, and when the price is higher, less so. (This somehow is not true of handbags and women's designer clothes, which seem to function counter to this rule.)

When interest rates are low, the price of renting money is low, and thus more people rent money. When they rent money, they usually do something with it. Most of them spend it; a few of them invest it. Either way, that rented money is newly created and deployed out into the economy, which helps to drive up prices and stimulate growth.

Conversely, when interest rates are high, the cost of renting money is higher and thus fewer people are willing to pay it. This reduces the amount of money moving around the system and available for deployment on lesser valued projects. One of the criticisms of an easy money policy is that it tends to allocate capital to projects that would not otherwise have been funded, and thus ultimately fail once a low interest rate environment has abated. This is why we see so many bankruptcies during periods of recession, which invariably follow a period of rising rates.

EXPANDING THE BALANCE SHEET

Besides you, me, and our fellow taxpayers who are footing all the expenses, there are three major parties involved in our economy: Congress, the Treasury, and the Federal Reserve. The first two were instituted at the beginning of our Republic, the latter was added in 1913 during Woodrow Wilson's administration, ostensibly to protect the public. Here is how it all goes down:

Step 1: Congress spends more than it can pay for, and so we have more costs (through spending and entitlements, etc.) than we have income (through taxes and tariffs, etc.)

Step 2: Congress borrows as much as it can through the issuance of bonds, called Treasuries.

Step 3: Once we have run out of countries and others who will loan us money, the Treasury turns to the Fed. The Treasury issues bonds (more Treasuries) to the Federal Reserve which then prints (electronically creates) dollars that the Fed exchanges for these bonds. This is called expanding the balance sheet, or buying bonds, or quantitative easing, or stimulus—anything but the most commonly understood term, printing money.

Step 4: Now that the Treasury has the newly created money, it is then free to distribute it per Congress' instructions. This is how Social Security, Medicare, Medicaid, the military industrial complex, and the interest on our ever-increasing debt gets paid.

Step 5: This newly created money is now out in the economy, where it is subjected to the Mandrake Mechanism (to be discussed shortly).

And here is the Monetary Base:

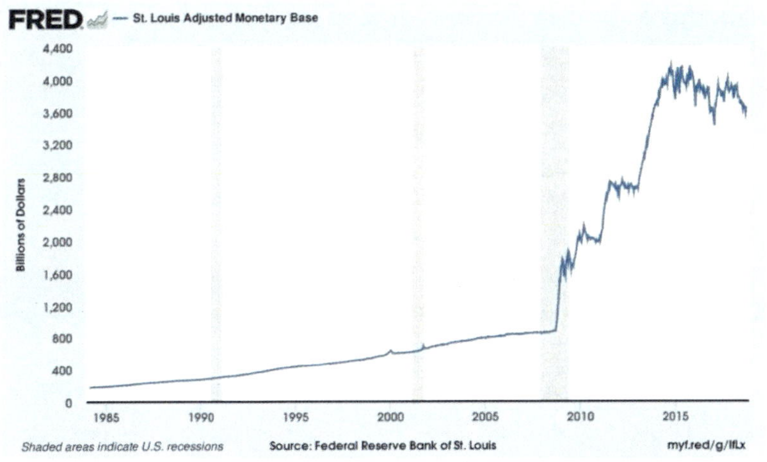

[14]

You can see the huge stimulus during the recession, and you can also see it beginning to unwind after 2015 as the Fed

[14] https://fred.stlouisfed.org/series/BASE (Set to Max)

attempts to reduce their balance sheet. Since this is such an unusual reaction to a market bust, it is uncertain as to how much this reduction will affect the markets, since most of this money is still on deposit with the Fed.

Nonetheless, it is the relativity of the longtime gentle slope juxtaposed with the extreme and violent infusion of money that I want to point out. I think it's hard to miss.

THE IMPORTANCE OF THE MANDRAKE MECHANISM

No matter where you live in the country, if you look around it shouldn't take too long to see the tell-tale signs of growth. Look for building cranes, highway construction, new office buildings, subdivisions, condos, grocery stores, retail outlets, new bridges, Starbucks locations, Wal-Mart supercenters. The list goes on.

Whenever you see these signs, I want you to immediately think this phrase: "monetary expansion." That's exactly what it is. Very few of these projects are paid for with money that already exists. Rather, our fractional reserve banking system is designed to "create" money when loans are advanced.

In his enlightening book, *The Creature from Jekyll Island*, G. Edward Griffin coins the term "Mandrake Mechanism" to describe this funny-money effect. The curious free-thinker should Google this term for some great YouTube videos that more artfully explain the process, but essentially it goes something like this:

Customer 1 deposits $100 into her account at Bank 1. Bank 1 then can lend out 90% of that $100. Customer 2 borrows $90 and deposits it into Bank 2, which can then loan out $81 to Customer 3. Bank 3 can then lend out $72.90 to Customer 4, who in turn deposits it into Bank 4. Bank 4 loans out $65.61 to Customer 5.... and on and on until we have gone 87 iterations, down to 1 cent. The total money created from the 87 deposits and loans is over $900. So, you can see how

$100 can turn into $900 through this Mechanism, especially if the reserve is lowered below its current ten percent.[15] So far, there have been no adjustments to the reserve requirements.

And here is another important takeaway: Just as this money can expand and grow on a logarithmic basis when we are in expansion mode, so it may unwind just as quickly and dramatically when we are in contraction mode, when it is oftentimes accompanied by a panic, which only exacerbates the meltdown when it finally comes.

OUR HOUSE OF CARDS

Despite the eventual unwinding, the result of all this monetary expansion creates an initial appearance and sense of real growth and prosperity. After all, we all want new and better roads and bridges and nice shiny new buildings. But this illusion of prosperity is just that—illusory.

I believe history has proven that eventually, inevitably, the "stimulus" of newly created money always collapses upon itself. You can call this "monetary contraction" and I liken it to a house of cards. If you slowly pull out cards one at a time, there will come a point when the entire thing collapses. You never know exactly which card will be the coup de grâce, but you know it's just a matter of time.

And so, my friends, that is where we are today. Perhaps you remember 2006. Remember all the growth, the cranes, the new buildings, et cetera? Well, welcome back. Then, of course, surely you remember 2008 and the market crash that erased trillions of dollars of value and witnessed the stock and real estate markets plunge by 35% or more.

This is your wake-up call. I'm sad to say, those days are coming again.

Who is the culprit in all this? The same culprit responsible

[15] This is an oversimplification. The true math is more complex, but for our purposes of example it is sufficient.

for the Great Depression: The Federal Reserve Bank. That's according to former Fed Chairman Ben Bernanke when, on November 8, 2002, in a speech given at a conference to honor Milton Friedman on his 90th birthday, Bernanke admits: "Regarding the Great Depression, … we did it. We're very sorry. … We won't do it again."[16]

They are the ones manipulating the money supply. It is they who created the real estate bubble; it is they who caused the crash in 2008. They are the ones who have created all this easy money with their zero-interest rate policy—which they call "stimulus"—and they are the ones who are now reversing course, pulling the cards out one by one. You can bet it's just a matter of time.

If you look at the next chart you can see that the Fed has raised the Fed Funds Rate already from roughly .1% to 1.5%. The rate that was required to crash the market in 2008 was 5.25%. We worry the rate to crash the current market bubble will be closer to 4%, or perhaps even 3%. You can see that we are almost half way there.

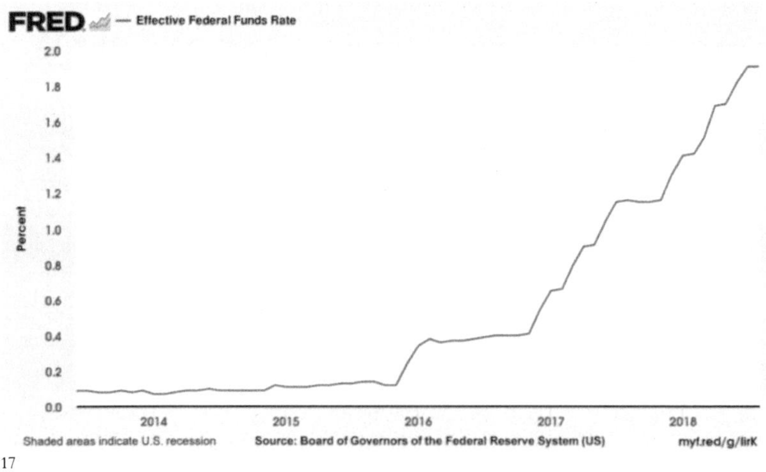

[17]

It won't happen overnight, and no one will know exactly

[16] https://www.federalreserve.gov/BOARDDOCS/SPEECHES/2002/20021108/
[17] https://fred.stlouisfed.org/series/DFF (Set to 5Y)

when it will occur, but rest assured, another correction is on the way. Ironically, some of the most substantial growth can occur in the run-up to a crash. Just look at the growth that occurred in 1998 and 1999, and again in 2006 and 2007. This is where we believe we are today.

Our expectation is that stocks and real estate will continue to run until… dramatically, and without warning, another 2000 or 2008-style crash occurs. If you have real estate or other investments that you feel have "peaked out," you may want to start thinking about divesting.

V

CRASH SIGNALS TO WATCH

After the 2016 presidential election the market took off—mainly due to the promise and probability of a corporate tax decrease. By the time the tax bill was signed in late December 2017, most of the growth had already occurred, but it wasn't until February 2018 that the market started to stutter. On February 5, Jerome Powell was sworn in as the new Fed Chairman, replacing Janet Yellen. On the very same day, the Dow Jones Industrials dropped over 4 percent.

It is not uncommon for the market to drop after the coronation of a new Fed chair. In fact, "the S&P 500 has fallen on the first days of the past couple of Fed chairs. Powell's first day coincided with a 4.1 percent drop. The index fell 0.9 percent on Yellen's first day, and it was down 2.2 percent on Ben Bernanke's first day."[18]

Powell's entry onto the scene is also a harbinger of higher rates and further tightening—exactly the kind that, in the past, has caused large market corrections. Nonetheless, we continue to believe that stocks, particularly large cap value stocks, could run another 20% as the corporate tax breaks reach the corporate bottom lines. We expect dividend increases, stock buy backs, and even special dividends. Thus, assuming as we do that stocks will recover from the initial new Fed chairman personality shock, the question becomes "How much higher can we go before the inevitable bust?"

---

[18] https://www.cnbc.com/2018/02/05/markets-putting-powell-to-the-test-even-quicker-than-other-fed-chairs.html

That's right, what we've experienced so far this year is a retrenchment—not a bust. As I write this, we are about 1600 points shy of our all-time high. I expect us to break through this before the end of summer 2018, and possibly much sooner. Of course, as I have been saying throughout this book, I expect the end of an incredible market run is likely to coincide with a massive 2008-style crash. Ironically, the recent retrenchment will likely embolden future investment as the market "gets back on track" after our awkward honeymoon with Jerome Powell winds down and everyone settles back into normalcy.

This is not a warning of an imminent stock market correction, but merely a reminder that we need to start thinking about our exit strategies. As they say before takeoff, "take note of the exits—the closest one might be behind you."

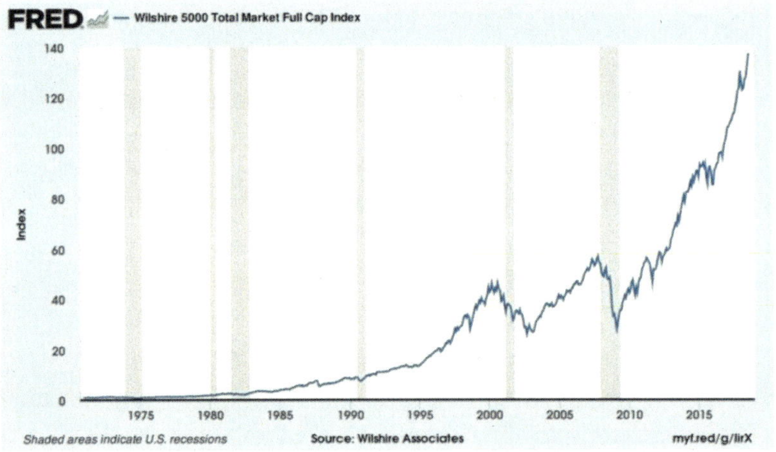

19

Preparing for the next stock market crash is not as easy as it seems, especially if there are tax ramifications. And, of course, the timing of it all. Strictly speaking, there is no proven method to successfully "time" the market—that is, buying in and selling out at exactly the right time and price. This is impossible, so it's futile to even try.

[19] https://fred.stlouisfed.org/series/WILL5000INDFC (Set to Max)

If your portfolio is up 100%, and you go into cash, then you have locked in that gain. Good for you. But what if your portfolio would have gained another 100% had you not gone into cash, and you have lingered there while earning nothing? What if, on the other hand, you had stayed completely invested and gained that additional 100%, but then lost 50%? Would you not be right back where you started, but with a lot more grey hair?

So, the goal is not to hit the mark exactly, but to lean to one side (the stock market) or the other (the bond market) as conditions dictate. What conditions, you ask? The conditions that we are looking for are essentially monetary expansion or contraction, and velocity—whether money is being created or destroyed, and how fast it's moving through the economy.

TRACKING THE FED FUNDS RATE

Take another look at the Fed Funds Rate chart on page 10. Since 1980, the rate needed to crash the market has been successively lower, so that all that was needed to cause the 2008 crash was a mere 5.25%. The next crash could occur at rates as low as 3%, there's just no way to know. But know this, if rates are north of 4% and the market hasn't yet crashed, then we'll be on the sidelines waiting for it.

In my opinion, the simplest way to "lean" out of stocks is to pick your warning rate, and then start slowly divesting every time the Fed raises rates. For example, let's take a client who was normally 70/30, meaning that 70% of her portfolio was in stocks and 30% in bonds and cash equivalents. (Every client's situation is different and this is just for demonstration purposes. Past performance is not indicative of future results.)

Beginning in late 2006, the Fed triggered our warning rate of 4%. Thereafter, each successive increase in the Fed Funds rate was followed by a 10% move from stocks to bonds. By the time March of 2008 came around, that same client's portfolio looked like 30/70, where only 30% was in the stock market. Obviously, this mitigated losses substantially.

Subsequently, after the market sustained between a 35% to 40% loss, we reversed the allocation to the original 70/30, buying up equities that we had previously sold only a year earlier, though at a significant discount. The unwinding effect of the Mandrake Mechanism is greatly exacerbated in times of panic, which is why market crashes happen so dramatically and suddenly.

The unmistakable trend has been a lower rate needed to crash the market, and a lower rate needed to stimulate the market. Notice that after the 2008 crisis our interest rate levels were barely floating above zero. I think next time you can expect something even more surprising: Negative Interest Rates.

THE SPECTER OF NEGATIVE INTEREST RATES

You read that right. Negative interest rates. Just when you thought the world couldn't get any weirder, it has. I can understand negative temperatures or negative press—but negative interest rates? That's a little like negative rain, or negative time. Nonetheless, they have arrived.

Sweden's central bank began the "experiment" in July 2009 in an effort to rejuvenate their economy after the 2008 crash. One might say that the Swedes invented it.[20] Of course, at the time, it didn't really make headline news because Sweden doesn't impact the world economy too terribly much. But since then, other desperate economies have started to use the stratagem: Large enough economies to shake the world markets.

[20] https://www.theguardian.com/business/2016/feb/18/negative-interest-rates-what-you-need-to-know

The first chart shows the Swiss banks going negative at the end of 2014 to almost minus 1% and sort of stabilizing a little under minus 0.7%.

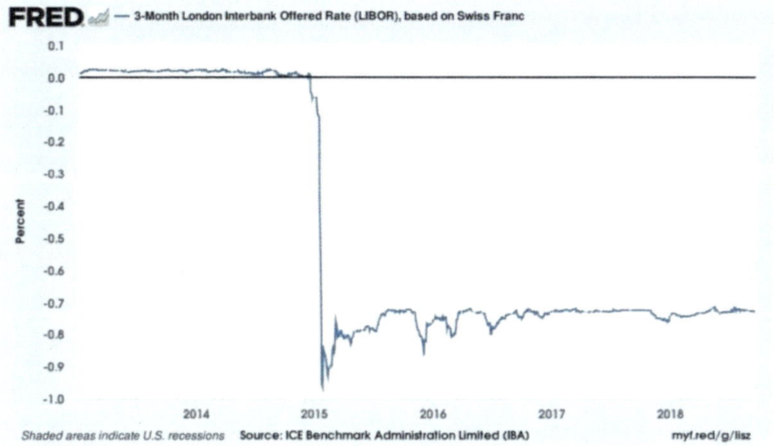

21

The next chart shows the European banks going negative in the middle of 2015, to about minus .25%.

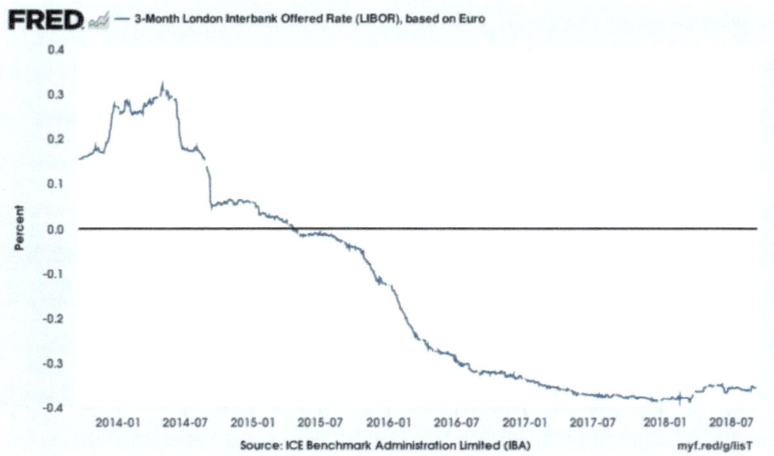

22

[21] https://fred.stlouisfed.org/series/CHF3MTD156N
[22] https://fred.stlouisfed.org/series/EUR3MTD156N

Not to be left to the European theater, the Japanese have imported negative rates to the Land of the Rising Sun. Here you can see Japan's rate going negative in the first quarter of 2016, down to just a fraction of a percent negative.

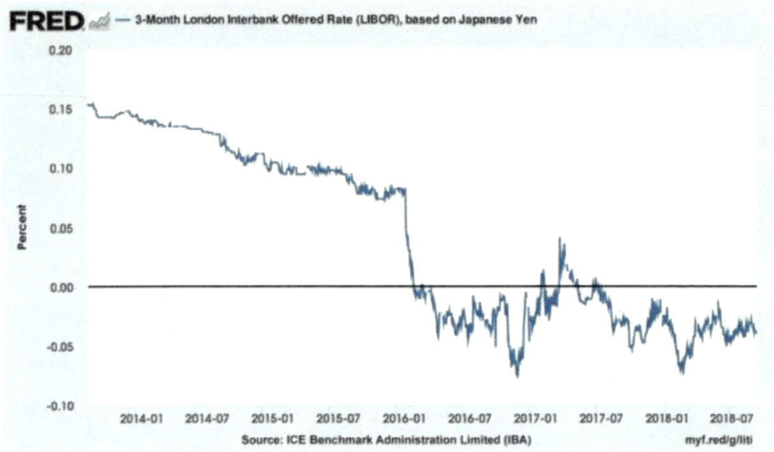

23

So out of the world's four largest economies, the European Union, the U.S., China, and Japan, two of them employ negative rates—Japan and the E.U. In all, there have been nine countries that have experimented with negative rates.[24] You know there is something very wrong with an economy when interest rates go negative. Can't you just intuitively *feel* that?

Who in their right mind would deposit money at a bank, and pay the bank interest? Already, we have seen where investors have begun to withdraw their cash rather than pay the negative interest. This has induced some lawmakers in Europe to consider getting rid of cash money altogether. According to the CFA Institute,

In early 2015, JPMorgan Chase forbade some customers from storing cash in safe deposit boxes. Swiss banks refused to allow pension funds to withdraw large amounts of cash from their accounts. Danish legislators proposed a law allowing

[23] https://fred.stlouisfed.org/series/JPY3MTD156N

[24] http://www.forbes.com/negative-interest-rates-coming-soon-to-a-bank-near-you

shops to refuse to accept cash payments. Australia imposed a 0.05% tax on some bank deposits. And France cut the legal limit on cash payments from 3,000 Euros to 1,000 Euros.[25]

The reason given by the European Central Bank for negative interest rates is "to further ease the already accommodative monetary policy stance to fight the growing threat of deflation amid downward pressures to inflation expectations."[26] In short, they want more inflation.

The lesson—like most economic lessons (as my econ professor Dr. Shropshire drilled into my psyche)—goes back to simple supply and demand.

Inflation comes simply from an increase in the money supply. The more money out in the economy, the less each unit of money is worth in terms of what you can buy. We can clearly see this in action at the grocery store, or in the price of stamps.

In utilizing negative rates, the central banks are trying to force people out of cash. They want you to spend it—which helps stock prices—and they want you to invest it, which also drives up stock prices. But most of all they want you to borrow it—because in a fractional-reserve banking system such as ours—borrowing actually "creates" money, and remember—more money means inflation.

Whatever the consequences of the negative interest rate experiment, we just don't believe it can be good in the long run. This completely undermines savers, and forces conservative investors into alternative products that carry too much risk. Everything is fine until it isn't.

If nothing else, we now know that zero is <u>not</u> the bottom, so the Fed is watching Europe and Japan with great interest. Perhaps they think they have another arrow in their quiver, to use when the market takes another 2008-style dive. I think you

---

[25] https://blogs.cfainstitute.org/how-will-negative-interest-rates-change-the-rules-of-the-game

[26] http://www.worldbank.org/Global-Economic-Prospects-June-2015-Negative-interest-rates

can bet on it.

We didn't see negative rates here in the U.S., but we sure got close. No, for us today, negative rates represent the *next* stimulus after the *next* bust following our *present* boom. Our immediate concern is when—or more precisely—at what rate, our current bull market will crash. For us at Magellan, our warning rate this time around is less than 4%, closer to 2.75%. After we hit this rate, we expect to start migrating out of everything except precious metals. But where do we go?

VI

SEEKING SAFETY IN AN UNSAFE WORLD

A close examination of the Great Recession of 2008 is quite revealing. Our intention, of course, was to scour the universe in search of an asset class that actually 'held up' during the 2008 crisis. Having lived through it, I can remember a time when AAA rated municipal bonds were down 35%. Is ANYTHING that is AAA rated EVER supposed to be down 35%?

Absolutely not. At most, in the worst crisis imaginable, AAA should be down no more than 7%. And that is on the outside. But there they were—AAA rated municipal bonds, down 35%! Amazing! Shocking! And terrifying. Can this happen again? Only a fool would say 'no'.

ASSET CLASSES MOVE IN CYCLES

Those AAA municipal bonds could have made you rich if you had had the courage to buy when everyone else was selling. All anomalies like that correct themselves over time, and a 35% discount on AAA bonds is unheard of. What an incredible opportunity. Several wily investors almost doubled their money and collected tax free interest of nearly 10% while they waited for the bonds to recover, which they did within eight months.

The chart on the following page looks a lot like the periodic table of the elements and may remind you of chemistry class, but it is really a colorful representation of the relative movements of the various asset classes. It ranks key indices in order of performance for the last twenty years.

Graphically, it is a great representation of movements of the asset classes. Note that each color represents a specific kind of investment type, such as **bright orange for emerging markets**, **gray for large cap value stocks** (S&P 500), and **light blue for the bond aggregate** (U.S. Fixed Income).

Focus for a moment just on the bright orange and the light blue. These represent the polar ends of the spectrum—bonds being the safest asset on the chart and emerging markets being the riskiest. Note how they often rotate from first to worst and back. Emerging markets were at the top in 2007, dropped to the bottom in 2008, with a 53% loss, only to be back on top in 2009. This pattern repeats itself in 2011-2013.

If you look at the light blue during those same periods, you will notice an almost opposite movement, with the bonds moving less dramatically. Since our raison d'être here is to protect our portfolios during the next market crash, we should focus in on 2008, since we are likely to see a year very similar to that within the not-too-distant future.

In 2008, you can see that everything was down significantly, except bonds. You see that in that year the bond aggregate actually gained 5.24%. But that doesn't tell the whole story, because the bond aggregate is an amalgamation of treasuries, investment grade corporate bonds, and mortgage-backed securities like Ginnie Maes. Also, that 5.24% was at the end of the year when most of the bonds had by then recovered. What that number doesn't reflect, however, is the tumultuous volatility and uncertainly that plagued the bond market in the interim.

Asset Class Returns

Annual Returns										
2007	2008	2009	2010	2011	2012	2013	2014	2015	2016	2017
Emerging Markets 39.38%	U.S. Fixed Income 5.24%	Emerging Markets 78.51%	Small Cap Growth 29.09%	U.S. Fixed Income 7.84%	Emerging Markets 18.23%	Small Cap Growth 43.30%	S&P 500 Growth 14.89%	S&P 500 Growth 5.52%	Small Cap Value 31.74%	Emerging Markets 37.28%
S&P 500 Growth 9.13%	High Yield Bonds -26.16%	High Yield Bonds 58.21%	Small Cap Value 24.50%	High Yield Bonds 4.98%	Small Cap Value 18.05%	Small Cap Value 34.52%	S&P 500 Value 12.36%	U.S. Fixed Income 0.55%	S&P 500 Value 17.40%	S&P 500 Growth 27.44%
Small Cap Growth 7.05%	Small Cap Value -28.92%	Small Cap Growth 34.47%	Emerging Markets 18.88%	S&P 500 Growth 4.65%	S&P 500 Value 17.68%	S&P 500 Growth 32.75%	U.S. Fixed Income 5.97%	Small Cap Growth -1.38%	High Yield Bonds 17.13%	Small Cap Growth 22.17%
U.S. Fixed Income 6.97%	S&P 500 Growth -34.92%	S&P 500 Growth 31.57%	High Yield Bonds 15.12%	S&P 500 Value -0.48%	High Yield Bonds 15.81%	S&P 500 Value 31.99%	Small Cap Growth 5.60%	S&P 500 Value -3.13%	Small Cap Growth 11.32%	S&P 500 Value 15.36%
S&P 500 Value 1.99%	Small Cap Growth -38.54%	S&P 500 Value 21.17%	S&P 500 Value 15.10%	Small Cap Growth -2.91%	S&P 500 Growth 14.61%	High Yield Bonds 7.44%	Small Cap Value 4.22%	High Yield Bonds -4.47%	Emerging Markets 11.19%	Small Cap Value 7.84%
High Yield Bonds 1.87%	S&P 500 Value -39.22%	Small Cap Value 20.58%	S&P 500 Growth 15.05%	Small Cap Value -5.50%	Small Cap Growth 14.59%	U.S. Fixed Income -2.02%	High Yield Bonds 2.45%	Small Cap Value -7.47%	S&P 500 Growth 6.89%	High Yield Bonds 7.50%
Small Cap Value -9.78%	Emerging Markets -53.33%	U.S. Fixed Income 5.93%	U.S. Fixed Income 6.54%	Emerging Markets -18.42%	U.S. Fixed Income 4.21%	Emerging Markets -2.60%	Emerging Markets -2.19%	Emerging Markets -14.92%	U.S. Fixed Income 2.65%	U.S. Fixed Income 3.54%

Sources: Bloomberg Barclays Aggregate U.S. Bond Index; Bloomberg Barclays Corp High Yield Bond Index; Morgan Stanley Capital International Index; Russell 2000 Small Capital Growth; Russell 2000 Small Capital Value; S&P 500 Growth; S&P 500 Value

[27]

[27] http://www.callan.com/periodic-table

The truth of the matter is this: when 2008 hit, investors the world over, institutional and individual, shunned every single asset class save one: U.S. treasuries. In fact, the 20-year treasury gained 33% that year. Of course, it gave most of that back in 2009. But other bonds—those that many thought were safe—were off dramatically. AAA rated municipals, as I mentioned before, and high-quality corporates, suffered significantly.

After scrutinizing what did well and what turned sour during the Great Recession, it turns out that only bonds backed by the U.S. Treasury held any demand: the 1-3-year treasuries, the 3-5-year treasuries, and 7-10-year treasuries. All of these fared well during the crash, and though they didn't gain a lot in 2009, at least they held on to their previous year's gain.

One strategy that an investor, who is worried about these issues, could take and that worked well during the Great Recession is to migrate into these three asset classes: very short, short, and medium-term treasuries. Rather than go through the hassle and cost of buying individual treasuries, an index fund works well enough, and with low expenses. Of course, past performance does not guarantee future results.

After World War I, the U.S. dollar became the world's reserve currency, supplanting Great Britain's sterling. Since then, whenever there is fear in the international markets, investors—mainly institutional—flood into treasuries because the U.S. dollar is seen as the safest currency on the planet. This was certainly true in 2008, and it continues to be true to this day.

Just for fun, pay attention to the correlation between world news events, stock market movements, and the price (and yield) of treasuries. Generally, it goes something like this:

1. Bad international event, e.g., regional war, terrible catastrophe, sovereign debt crisis.
2. Investors sell their riskier positions which are usually in emerging markets.

3. Investors move that money into U.S. treasuries of various maturities. This drives up the price of treasuries.
4. Higher treasury prices drive down the yields on the treasuries.
5. Because investors cannot buy treasuries in anything other than dollars, the value of the dollar increases relative to other currencies.
6. When fear of the international event abates, the steps above reverse themselves.

This is the cycle, and until U.S. treasuries are no longer deemed safe, it will almost certainly continue. But there are concerns.

VII

OUR SOVEREIGN DEBT – THE REAL ENEMY

These charts represent *our* debt--the USA. The first chart to the right is our total public debt in terms of millions of dollars. In 1970, you can see it was practically nothing.

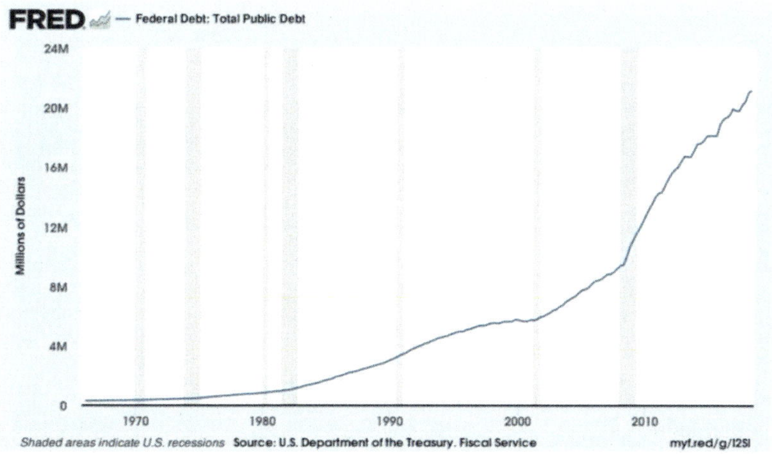

28

By 9/11, we were steady at around $6 trillion (shown as 6M millions of dollars). Today, our total debt is over a whopping 21 trillion. Do you think we will *ever* pay that off? What's worse, not only can we not pay it off, we can't even slow it down. Why is no one talking about this? This is the *real* danger to America.

Here's another way to look at debt—which is as a

[28] FRED, Federal Reserve Bank of St. Louis; https://fred.stlouisfed.org/series/GFDEBTN

percentage of Gross Domestic Product (GDP). This is helpful when comparing economies. So, for example, at 9/11 we had debt of only 55% of our economy. Today it is over 100%. How high can we go?

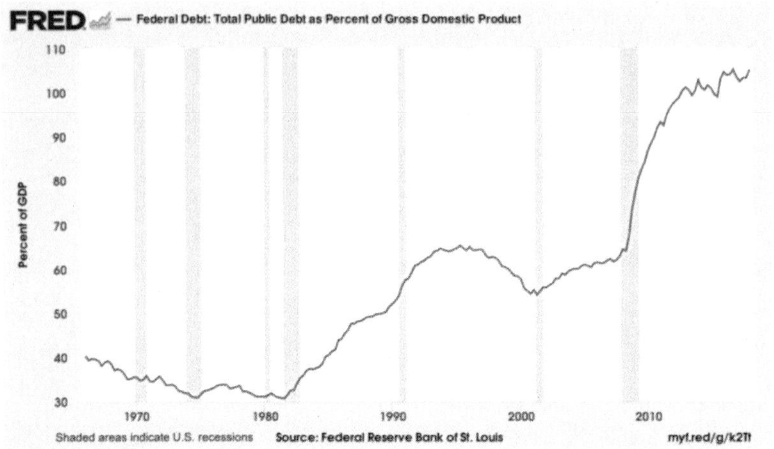

[29]

Other economies fare worse. Greece, for instance, has a debt to GDP ratio of closer to 160%. And Japan's debt to GDP ratio is over an astonishing 200%!

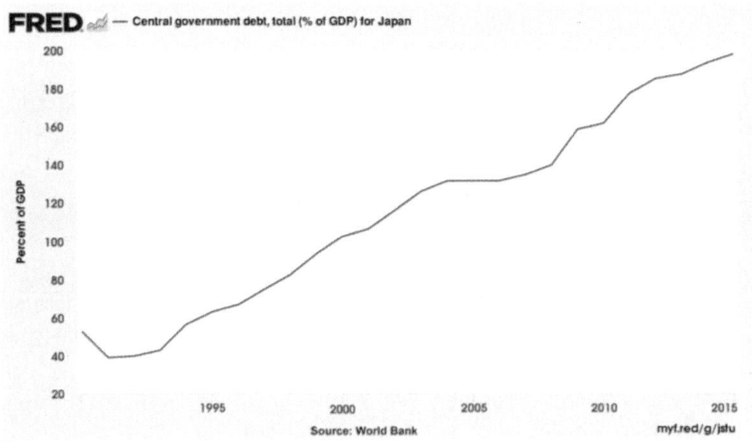

[30]

---

[29] https://fred.stlouisfed.org/series/GFDEGDQ188S

[29] https://fred.stlouisfed.org/series/DEBTTLJPA188A

It is in the interest of highly indebted countries (and people) to have inflation. In fact, the more inflation the better. Inflating money helps to drive down the "real" costs of debt. For example, a $1000 debt in 1920 was huge; today it's peanuts. So what does all this mean?

That's the million-dollar question. The rule of unintended consequences is surely to bite us in the end. And according to Austrian Economists like Professor Von Mises, unfettered inflation means an eventual end to the currency involved—even an international reserve currency like the great U.S. dollar.

My personal feeling is that the U.S. can go on like this for a while longer, and perhaps double our debt load to 200% of GDP as Japan is currently maintaining. Amazingly, not only are investors still buying Japanese bonds, but they are willing to pay the bank of Japan interest for the privilege to do so—those negative rates again. The next global recession could affect Japan's sovereign debt significantly. Will people still buy Japanese bonds?

And if investors are willing to buy Japanese bonds at negative rates with a 200% debt to GDP ratio, then one would suppose that investors will continue to buy U.S. debt with our debt to GDP at "only" 100%, even with our bonds paying practically nothing.

Of course, history is replete with false assumptions and dire mistakes. Historically, if the world fiat currencies finally do fail, there is but one proven alternative: precious metals.

VIII

PHYSICAL BULLION

Gold and silver and other precious metals have always held a special place in the history and economies of myriad cultures of our human race. Even from the earliest known times, the veneration of these shiny metals has been global. But have you ever wondered why? The answer is surprisingly cosmic.

Our sun, the small to medium-sized star on which our very lives depend, is a third-generation star. It was born from an immense gaseous cloud of what had been an explosion of an earlier star, itself reborn from an even earlier explosion. The death of stars is something special, and the mass of a star during its life will dictate its death, which can be spectacular to truly inconceivable. A star is essentially a struggle between nuclear fusion pushing outwards and the forces of gravity pushing inwards. When the fusionable material is finally exhausted, gravity will eventually win. It always does. And this is when the mass of the star dictates its destiny.

"Ordinary" stars like our sun will sort of hemorrhage toward the end and then fizzle out into what's called a "white dwarf." "Super massive" stars, greater than 260 times our sun, will completely collapse upon their own weight, and rip the very fabric of space-time, becoming super-massive black holes. Scientists now believe there is one of these massive beasts at the center of every galaxy. And our solar system, two-thirds out on a spiral arm, is just being tugged along its immense gravitational spin.[31]

"What does any of this have to do with anything at all related to gold or silver?" Great question. But please bear with me, as the answer lies in another type of stellar death that occurs when stars aren't too small or too large, but just right—the Goldilocks star.

These stars go supernova. Which means that once they begin to collapse from their own weight, molecules are fused together to create completely new elements—heavier and heavier—until eventually iron emerges. Once this stage is reached, mere moments elapse before an explosion—the likes of which you can't imagine—spews pure energy, light, gas, and dust for light years in every direction. During this massive explosion, with pressures too immense to properly measure, the remnants of the star's iron are further refined. Slammed together at nearly the speed of light, the shards of iron produce all of the universe's heavy (and sometimes radioactive) elements—lead, mercury, even uranium. But this intergalactic explosion also produces something else. Some-thing heavier than iron, but not radioactive: gold, silver, and platinum.

And so there, in the death throes of a 4-billion-year-old star—not too big, not too small—is where silver and gold are created. Something special for sure, and not easily duplicated. This is the main reason gold and silver have historically been a preferred form of storing wealth. This history was certainly known to our nation's Founders, who had witnessed many paper currencies devalue to nothing, as the phrase "ain't worth a continental" can attest. In fact, Article I, section 10 of the U.S. Constitution provides that "*[No State shall] make any Thing but gold and silver Coin a Tender in Payment of Debts;*" Unfortunately, this rule has been interpreted to include all of the states but not the federal government itself. Gold is therefore one of the chief indicators the Federal Reserve (and everyone else) monitors to gauge the current level of inflation.

---

[31] Gsfc.nasa.gov. National Aeronautics and Space Administration.

The following chart compares the price of gold (in dollars per ounce) to our monetary base (in red). Note that they tracked along more or less in tandem. But then on Wednesday, October 3, 2012 gold prices started to tumble. And three months later, on January 4, 2013, the Fed started pumping more money into the economy. Which is to say, created it from nothing.

32

Finally, the price of gold and the monetary base crossed over on Friday, May 24, 2013. It has remained upside down ever since. Theories abound as to the true cause of this price anomaly, but most agree that "something is rotten in the state of Denmark." A dramatic price drop in gold as we've seen would seemingly indicate a likewise dramatic decrease in gold demand. But the opposite seems to be the case. In fact, China's net imports of gold in 2013 were about 1,160 tons, double the amount they imported in 2012.[33]

That's over 37 million ounces. And this is *in addition to* all the gold that China refines domestically, which is unreported and unverifiable.

In any event, the sharp drop in the price of gold after

---

32 https://myf.red/g/liwp

33 Reuters. *China allows gold imports via Beijing, sources say, amid reserves buying talk.* 4/20/2014

October 3, 2013 runs counter to the historical trend of increasing prices as the money base is expanded. Something doesn't add up. Perhaps what has been going on in the silver market can help us understand what may be going on in the gold market. The silver market is more transparent because it is much more thinly traded, and more difficult and less affordable to transport globally, or even domestically.[34]

But like most commodities, one does not need to buy or sell the actual silver to profit from its price movement. There is an entire industry betting on the future price of many commodities like gold and silver, wheat, orange juice and even bacon.

A futures option "call" allows the buyer to pre-choose a maximum price at which she may buy, and likewise an option "put" allows the buyer to pre-choose a minimum price at which she may sell. Of course, on the other side there is the seller of the option, who must honor his side of the contract, to buy or sell when the option holder's price is reached. Futures options contracts can seem confusing because you're buying and selling the right and obligation to buy and sell, at some point in the future.

Even more confusing is the ability to "sell short." That is, to sell something *now* that you don't actually own—yet. Let's say I sell 100 tons of wheat at $500 per ton to be delivered in 1 year. I've already sold the wheat, but I don't actually have it. In fact, no one does, it hasn't even been sown, much less reaped. Next year when the wheat is due, I'm hoping the wheat will be selling for less than $500 per ton, say $400. In this way I have made a profit by selling at a higher price something which I can later substitute for a lower price.

This is similar to what has happened with silver. Someone, or perhaps several "someones," started selling silver short in massive quantities using these paper contracts. Meaning, they have been selling contracts representing physical silver that

---

[34] This is because the price per ounce of silver is much less than that of gold.

they don't own, and that doesn't even necessarily exist. And they didn't sell just a little, but nearly 172,000 contracts, each contract representing 5,000 ounces of silver bullion. That's over 860 million ounces that were sold (on paper) when only 60 million ounces were actually registered and available for delivery.[35] As of January 2018, there were over 196,000 outstanding silver futures contracts, representing 980 million ounces, and less than 46 million ounces registered and available for delivery.[36] The system works because very few contracts are ever actually "filled" or delivered. Most are closed out or expire worthless.

Movements in the dollar vis-à-vis other currencies are an illusory indicator of the "real" value of the dollar in the sense that it does not establish a true base line, as all major currencies are devaluing simultaneously, so any movement is merely *relative.* Only gold and silver are finite in their supply, having been born in the death throes of a Goldilocks supernova somewhere in a galaxy not too far away.

Nothing that I have told you is my original idea. Everything I have imparted I have learned from others, particularly the Austrian Economists. The Austrians believe in sound money, backed by gold and silver, and not the "funny money" that is so easily manufactured by those who have the exclusive license to do so.

But this is the economy in which we find ourselves, the economy in which we grew up. Not just domestically, but globally. We can be Austrians and believe in the value of a hard currency, but this is not what's accepted at McDonald's, or the IRS, or available in our 401k or IRA. And so, we have to play the Keynesian fiat game with the resources that are available to us. Which is to say, what do we do with our dollars?

Some Austrian school proponents would recommend dumping all dollars for the physical stuff, or to invest

---

[35] COMEX. CME Group. As of September 14, 2014.
[36] COMEX. CME Group. As of January 18, 2018.

everything in stocks and funds that are based on commodities. We do not subscribe to either of these drastic plans of action. In fact, there may be plenty of life left in our Keynesian economy after all, so there is no need to take any drastic action anytime soon. But with the price of gold and silver being so low, is it wise to hold onto it? Should we sell it and move on? On the contrary, what I see is a buyer's market. If silver and gold prices truly are being held artificially low, would you not expect the manipulators to be buying? Because they certainly are.

When I am buying gold or silver, I don't pay a numismatic value ("collector" prices)—I pay only for the value of the raw bullion. I also buy some "junk silver", which is pre-1965 U.S. minted dimes, quarters, and half-dollars. These coins certainly aren't "junk", but have a silver content of "only" 90%. They are usually available on-line or from bullion dealers.

In my opinion, when it comes to silver bullion, nothing beats silver eagles from the U.S. Mint. You will pay a premium for them over Canadian or South African or even Austrian silver, but they are well known among international silver dealers and simple country farmers alike. Again, the date of the coin, its mint run, and the nice plastic cases—I don't care about any of that. I just want the bullion.

WHERE DO I HOLD MY STASH?

I get this question all the time, and the answer I give immediately is: "anywhere but the bank!" When you need your bullion the most, the banks will be closed, as will be all financial institutions. The ATMs will not work. Credit cards will not work. EBT will not work.

I often recommend investing in a very secure home safe that is installed professionally and bolted to a concrete surface, like a basement or garage. Your safe should weigh about 700-1000 pounds and be bolted to a cement surface. Expect to pay around $1200-$1500 installed. Do not use an electronic lock, but rather the classic dial lock like you see in westerns. Finally, don't tell anyone where it is or divulge the combination (except to your trusted executor or successor trustee). The especially wily may consider a distraction safe that is obvious and poorly stocked, with the real safe safely disguised or hidden.

If that is not practicable, consider an off-site secure storage area. You may be able to fit a smaller safe in the corner and pile lots of junk on top of it, so that the average intruder would not be excited to rummage through it. The fewer people who know, the better.

ASSET ALLOCATION WILL ALWAYS MATTER

I want to make it clear that I am not advocating an abandonment of the sound principles of asset allocation and diversification. On the contrary, rebalancing your portfolio during times of extreme volatility is usually very beneficial.

Several countries have, in their history, changed from one currency to another. In south America, it happens all the time. This does not mean that the entire economy collapses. Things do go on. People continue to buy soap and toothpaste; they continue to pump gas; they even continue to go out to eat. It only means that the medium of exchange has changed.

Precious metals, and other real assets, tend to do very well during a currency crises, and may present an opportunity to rebalance into other assets that have slumped. Physical bullion is just one asset class among many, and I could never advocate investing more than ten percent (10%) of your entire net worth into any one asset class, including precious metals.

IX

WILL THE REAL INFLATION RATE PLEASE STAND UP?

Interestingly, and perhaps suspiciously, the price of silver (and gold) has historically been a good indicator as to the real rate of inflation. It is certainly one of the headline indicators that the Federal Reserve follows. A sharp decline in the precious metals market would indicate that inflation is low or perhaps flat. Conversely, a sharp increase in precious metals would indicate a concern of rising inflation.

As Mark Twain once said, "There are three kinds of lies: lies, damned lies, and statistics."[37] The official inflation rate, called the Consumer Price Index (CPI), is formulated and issued by the U.S. Bureau of Labor and Statistics (BLS), a government agency. It is curious to note that the formula for this Index was adjusted in 1980, and again in 1990. It was adjusted because no one liked what they saw.

A specialist in government statistics, John Williams continues to track and report the results of the old formulas on his site, Shadowstats.com. On the next page is the 1980-based CPI formula compared to the one used today.

[37] http://www.twainquotes.com/Statistics.html

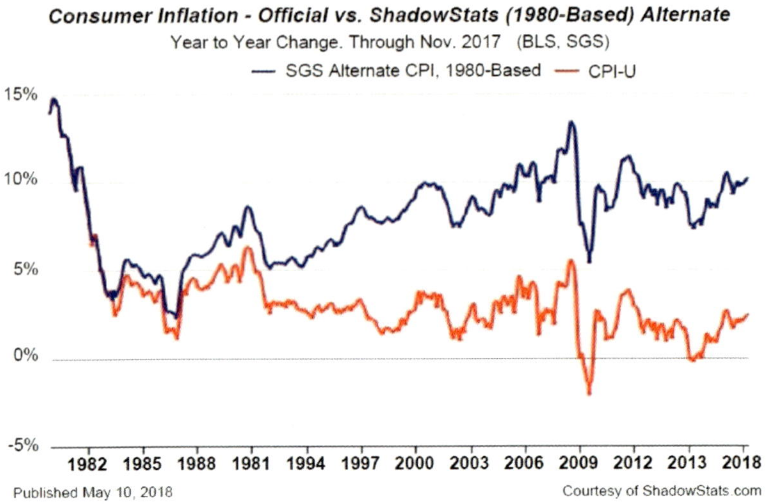

[38]

It's pretty obvious that if we were still using the 1980 formula, inflation today would be closer to 10%. This may be more consistent with your real-world experience with line items such as groceries, tuition, and healthcare costs.

Once you realize that the CPI is the number used to base social security cost of living increases to the millions and millions of social security recipients, it becomes understandable why the government would want to finagle with the numbers. But is that really fair to all of those who paid into the system all during their working life and now depend on it for sustenance during their retirement?

We believe inflation could become worse in the coming years, and those precious metals may rise significantly in value vis-à-vis the ever-devaluing dollar. If things get bad enough, à la Weimer Republic or Venezuela or the like, then those precious metals may become a temporary currency until the dollar can be replaced, most likely with the Special Drawing Right (SDR), to be discussed shortly. Unlikely, yes, but

[38] John Williams' Shadow Government Statistics, https://www.shadowstats.com/alternate_data/inflation-charts

impossible?

Nonetheless, it doesn't hurt to have a backup plan just in case. History has proven, to me at least, that there is a good case for holding precious metals, both as an investment and as an inflation hedge. We don't know when the price of precious metals will spike, only that history repeatedly implies that one day they may. It could be that the impetus will be the coming market crash and subsequent recession.

X

THE TRUTH ABOUT ANNUITIES

There's a character on TV who hates annuities—absolutely hates them. Maybe you've seen him. He says he "would rather die and go to hell than to sell an annuity." He actually says that. On another commercial, he claims also to be a fiduciary. Obviously, it never occurred to him that these two statements are mutually exclusive: you can't be acting in a fiduciary capacity if you have already discarded an entire set of asset classes *a priori*. Because when you exclude all annuities, you have excluded immediate annuities, fixed annuities, indexed annuities, and variable annuities. And each of these is really a different asset class, with different risk/return characteristics. My grandmother, for example, who turns 102 this June, would have run out of money long ago if it had not been for her annuity—her immediate annuity.

Like our comical TV character, one constantly hears about the horrible attributes of annuities and how the expenses are too high to justify the tax deferral or death benefit features that annuities can sometimes provide. At the same time, one cannot discount the fact that Americans have invested trillions of dollars in annuities. Can that many people, people with money, all be wrong—or have made a stupid mistake?

Here are some truisms about annuities upon which you can depend:

> **Truism 1**: Some people who own annuities do not understand what it is that they actually own.

Truism 2: Some people who are selling annuities do not understand what they are actually selling.

Truism 3: Some annuities are sold mainly because of their high commissions. Sad, but true.

Truism 4: Because of Truisms 1, 2 & 3, some people who own annuities bought them on false assumptions.

Truism 5: Many people who could benefit from owning an annuity do not because of the unprecedented confusion surrounding the investment.

Truism 6: Most people who comment or advise others on annuities, do not really understand the myriad of complex benefits and pitfalls of every existing annuity from every company with every possible option in every possible situation.

Truism 7: The term "annuity" is over-extended in its definition as an investment conduit.

Truism 8: Prospectuses and so-called disclosure statements are rarely read, and very difficult for the average person to understand.

Truism 9: The division of jurisdiction of regulatory authority between the Feds and the states creates a "gray area" of regulation, or lack thereof.

Nonetheless, annuities can have a place in certain situations. But they can also be complex, confusing, and often misunderstood—and sometimes misrepresented.

The most significant factor in understanding the general public's epic confusion regarding annuities is that every single investment product offered by an insurance company—that is not actually insurance—falls under the nebulous classification of "annuity." What is an "annuity?" Ask fifty people and you will get fifty different answers. Let us first start with the basics.

Obviously, most public insurance companies offer stock, preferred stock, bonds, notes, et cetera. These are investment conduits <u>in</u> the company, however, and are not products <u>of</u> the insurance company, just as they are not the *product* of *any* company, but a form of ownership or indebtedness of the company.

Thus, in theory at least, the life insurance industry has basically two classifications of products: Life insurance and annuities. These two general types of products are limited to insurance companies because both require the use (or potential use) of mortality tables. Insurance companies employ actuaries who use statistical data from actual experience to predict future experience, and thus interpolate and extrapolate this information to estimate the financial reserves needed to cover expected, impending liabilities, plus a little extra for profit.

Mortality tables are beneficial for determining how much money should be paid in premiums over time in order to provide a lump sum payment in the future, at a more or less expected date, i.e. life insurance. Mortality tables can also work in reverse, by calculating the lump sum of money required today that will provide for a series of payments to last for as long as the insured lives, which has a more or less expected date, e.g. annuities. This is like life insurance in reverse—where instead of making payments for a lump sum, you pay a lump sum to receive payments. Both calculations are based on your expected mortality, or more plainly, on how long people just like you are expected to live, based on how long people just like you (or similar to you) have been living.

The word "annuity" derives from the Latin base "*anno*," which means "year" or "annual," as in "*Anno Domini*"—or, "the Year of our Lord." This term is believed to have been adopted by the Knights Templar, who evolved to become the first central bank of Medieval Europe, and indeed all of Christendom.

In its purest form, an annuity makes a payment once per year until the annuitant, the person upon whose life the payment is based, dies. Upon death, no more payments are made, and the insurer (the annuity obligor), keeps whatever lump sum was paid up front by the annuitant.

The obligor (insurance company) is taking a risk, however, because the annuitant may live well passed his or her expected age, and the obligor must pay and pay and pay for as long as the annuitant lives. It is not enough that the obligor could not foresee revolutionary medical breakthroughs—this is the risk the obligor takes. Thus, in effect, an annuitant has shifted the risk of living longer than expected to the insurance company, just as the owner of a life insurance policy has shifted the risk of premature death.

The Knights Templar's presence in southern France led to the annuity's more common use as a "pension"—which is essentially an annuity that is paid monthly. It may be easier to think of a traditional annuity as a pension, because that's what it is: a series of payments to be paid for life. This is also sometimes called an "immediate annuity," an "annuitized annuity," or simply just "annuity." When most people hear the word "annuity," this is generally what comes to mind. In fact, most annuities today <u>could not be more different</u> than this "pension" ancestor, though all annuities could be converted to an annuitized annuity. This is the one thing they all have in common, and why they all share the same ambiguous name.

IMMEDIATE ANNUITIES

As we have seen, the immediate annuity is useful in alleviating the risk of living too long. Just as insurance companies insure against the possibility of living too briefly, a life annuity insures against the potentiality of living too long—or more specifically, beyond one's income resources. Take my grandmother as an example again. When she was 78, we had a family meeting and discussed putting a large chunk of her investable estate in an immediate annuity. The annuity had a provision that it would pay Grandma for life, but if she happened to die within the first ten years, the annuity payments would be made to her children instead. We knew that Grandma's father had lived until 96, and that her health was outstanding. She took no medication and had never known the taste of alcohol. She was the perfect candidate for an immediate annuity—and she really was. She has already seen her life expectancy come and go, and she still gets those monthly checks. When Grandma dies, her payments will finally end, and her beneficiaries will receive nothing. But for Grandma, it was the right thing to do. She had no market risk, and her longevity risk was essentially eliminated. The Great Recession came and went, and she never even knew it.

Because all this risk is being shifted to an insurance company, it's important to find one that's reputable and financially sound, with significant surplus reserves. This means that if all the company's liabilities come due at once—a worst case scenario—then the company has enough assets to pay them all off, and still be left with billions of dollars.

So that's an immediate annuity, meaning that the annuitant (or owner) begins taking payments immediately. The other general type of annuity is where the annuitant is not taking payments, but deferring them. Thus, the deferred annuity.

DEFERRED ANNUITIES

The thing to remember about deferred annuities is that the money invested (they call it a premium, which also confuses people) can be exposed to growth through three basic mechanisms, but in every case the income is deferred until the owner decides to start taking annuity payments. The three kinds of deferred annuities are essentially differentiated by the underlying investment 'engine' within each.

1. Fixed Annuities

Fixed annuities are relatively simple. A fixed rate for a fixed term. Though not 100% accurate, they are sometimes thought of as a CD replacement. For example, with a five-year fixed annuity yielding 4%, you put your money in, you earn 4% for five years, and when it's over, you take your money back and do something else. Simple. Sure, you *could* annuitize it, but most people don't.

Often, fixed annuities have a term of three to ten years. Five to seven years is the most common. During this period of time you will pay a penalty (somewhere between 2 to 10%) if you withdraw all of your money at once. Generally, you are allowed up to 10% per year as a free withdrawal, but this is not always so. Additionally, the fixed interest rate period may not be the same as the penalty period, so you need to be sure that you know what your guarantees are.

The rates in fixed annuities are low, also like CDs. But they are typically considered safe, and the interest is tax deferred, meaning that you pay no taxes on any growth until you withdraw it. This is true of all deferred annuities. And as a rule of thumb, it's worst out, first out. Meaning that you must take out (and pay taxes on) the growth before you can get down to your cost basis, which comes back to you as a return of after-tax dollars.

But growth in annuities is not subject to capital gains taxes when withdrawn; the growth is considered ordinary income when withdrawn, which in some cases could be worse. In a qualified account like an IRA or SEP this is immaterial, but for non-qualified (after-tax) accounts, this could create a higher tax bracket than you otherwise would have had if you had been subject to long term capital gains treatment instead. In order to do this, you would have to stick with stocks, mutual funds, and ETFs, and all the market risk that comes with them. There is always a trade-off.

2. **Indexed Annuities**

An indexed annuity also usually starts out as a deferred annuity, with the investment (premium) guaranteed against any market losses. That's good, but the trade-off is that your upside potential earnings are limited. An indexed annuity pays interest based on the performance of an index. Most indexed annuities utilize the S&P 500, but other major indices are often available, such as the Nasdaq, the Russell 2000, and the Hang Seng. With some annuities, you can even split your investment between multiple indices.

The two most common types of crediting strategies are a "capped point-to-point", and a "participation rate." A capped point-to-point is simple enough: Take the value of a given index on Day 1 and then compare it with the value of the same index on Day 366. Whatever percentage increase that represents is the rate of interest that is applied to your investment—up to a cap. For instance, let's say you invested $100,000 on January 1 and the index was 1000. Exactly one year later, the index had increased to 1100, an increase of 10%. You would receive this percentage, up to your cap. If your cap is 8%, you will receive 8%, if your cap is 12%, you will receive 10%.

Another popular interest crediting strategy is the participation rate. Like it sounds, you have a ratio at which you get to participate in the growth of an index. In the case above, with a 10% increase in the index (instead of a cap like 8%) you would have a rate of participation like 60%. That means that your credited interest rate will be equal to 60% of the growth of the index, in this case 10%. Thus, your actual net credited interest rate would be 6% (60% of 10%).

But what if the index were to drop substantially during the same time period? In that case you didn't earn anything, but you also didn't lose anything. And in years like 2008, no loss is a big win. So you can see the trade-off: you are giving up the opportunity of large gains so that your principal and your prior years' earnings are protected against future loss. I think that's pretty fair. However, it must be said that there are also some annuity products that I do not believe should be purchased by anyone. These are often shrouded in complexity and too-good-to-be-true promises from eager salespeople.

Like most deferred annuities, you will have a surrender period, and usually indexed annuities require a seven to ten-year commitment. Another point to be cognizant of is that the insurance companies reserve the right to change these rates, and they often do. For instance, the caps used to be around 10%, whereas the current caps are closer to 6%; and the participation rates are closer to 40%, when in earlier days I saw them as high as 90%. Much of this is driven by interest rates and the price of call and put options, since the insurers are using derivatives to hedge part of their exposure to extreme market volatility. An experienced financial advisor can explain these hedge strategies to you or you may decide that you don't need to worry about any of that. Like some of my clients who drive very expensive cars, they don't care to look under the hood.

3. Variable Annuities

There is no doubt that variable annuities are one of the most complex and varied financial instruments on the planet. It takes four licenses to sell them: you need a state-issued insurance license, a state-issued variable license, *and* federal and state securities licenses. This means that variable annuities fall under the purview of not just the individual states, but also the Feds, through FINRA[39] and the SEC.[40] What this means from my experience is that these annuities, though relatively expensive, are not predatory in the way some of the indexed annuities can be, which of course are not regulated by the Feds. For example, rarely would you ever find a variable annuity with a surrender period longer than ten years, but I have seen indexed annuities with eighteen-year surrender periods, and twenty percent surrender penalties.

So variable annuities, being regulated as securities under federal securities laws, come with a prospectus, and can only be sold by licensed FINRA representatives, which I can tell you from personal experience, are much, much more highly regulated. Beware, however; this does not mean that they are suitable for your situation. In today's regulatory environment, there is a need to prove that a variable annuity is suitable.

---

[39] FINRA - Financial Industry National Regulatory Authority.

[40] SEC – The United States Securities and Exchange Commission.

Again, this improvement is driven by the Feds.

Variable annuities are the only annuities in which you can lose money due to market loss. The reason for this is that your investment (premium) can be allocated among different sub accounts, which are a lot like mutual funds. In fact, it is often mutual fund companies who are managing these sub accounts, intending to "mirror" one of their more popular retail mutual funds. And just like mutual funds, they can hold stocks and commodities, or they can hold corporate bonds and treasuries. This is where the variable part comes into play. And also, higher expenses. I suspect our aforementioned annuity-hater is probably thinking about this version of the annuity, and in some cases, he has a point. But, again, a fiduciary must be able and willing to consider all available options.

It is true that variable annuities generally have higher expenses than a typical mutual fund, mainly because you have another layer of fees; but you may also have some type of additional rider that justifies the extra expense, such as a death benefit or a living benefit, or possibly both. There are a few living benefits that may make sense in some cases. For example, I bought two variable annuities for myself. But in my mind, they're not really for me, they're for my wife. She is younger than me and statistics show that she is highly likely to not only outlive me, but to live to be a centurion like my grandmother.

My annuities are expensive, no doubt, but I do not have a guaranteed pension like my grandparents did, and all my other investments are in some way, shape or form tied to the markets, so I was willing to bear additional costs for some insurance on this portion of my money. My money is invested in sub accounts that are aggressive, but I am totally unconcerned about a market crash, because I have a guarantee that provides a "living benefit" to me and my wife no matter how long we live. This benefit grows with the market and "locks in" every quarter, so subsequent losses cannot decrease my benefit. In fact, no matter what happens to my sub accounts (and they can drop just like anything else) my living benefit not only avoids losses, it continues to grow at a net rate of 6%.

Sound too good to be true? No, but it *is* too good to be cheap. I know what I'm paying; but I also know what I'm getting. So, what *am* I paying? Each sub account has a different expense ratio, with fixed income being the cheapest and small caps and international stocks and emerging markets the most expensive. In general, I'm paying an average of 1% there. Then, I have the cost of the annuity itself, which is 1.3%. They call this an "M&E" fee, or "Mortality and Expense Risk" fee. And then, on top of all that, I have the rider charge, which is the insurance on my money. This fee is about 1.5%. So, if you add it all up, I'm a tad under 4%. Not cheap. But on the other hand, I don't have to allocate as much money to the fixed income portion and can be more aggressive knowing that I have a minimum of 6% growth on my living benefit.

Here again is a trade off—if my funds were to gross 12%, I would receive roughly 8% growth in my subaccounts and my living benefit due to the fees. However, if the market drops 12%, my subaccounts will drop likewise, but my living benefit will increase by a net of 6%. This is a function of the living benefit that I am paying for—insurance against loss or poor performance—and it will eventually pay me back, but more importantly, it will pay my wife for the rest of her life, no matter how long she lives.[41]

Clearly, I don't have all of my money here, and as you know I'm a big proponent of silver, but I don't have all of my money there either. I have diversified, and I urge you to do the same. Having some money in one of these types of annuities isn't worth "condemning yourself to hell"; they can have a valid place in a world with fewer and fewer guarantees. And the few guarantees you do have come from a government with $21 trillion of debt and little hope of ever paying it off. To me,

---

[41] These guarantees are solely subject to the solvency of the insurance company ensuring the benefits.

that's no guarantee at all. Remember, surplus reserves.

One thing you can count on with the insurance industry is that they will do whatever it takes to keep up a good reputation—since so much of their business is built on trust. If one insurance company has trouble, the others swoop in (usually under state supervision) and pick up the policyholders of the faltering company. In this way, no insurance contracts (which must always remain sacrosanct as public policy) have ever been breached. This unspoken rule goes back centuries. Even during the Civil War there are stories of insurance companies paying claims to beneficiaries on "the other side", against popular sentiment, in order to protect the reputation of the industry.

GENERAL ANNUITY ADVICE

The biggest problem I have with annuities is the commission. Commission creates an internal and substantial conflict of interest. These "Voodoo 500" indexed annuities that have surrender periods of fifteen plus years with penalties reaching twenty percent can be so complex and confusing that the rosy promises of the salesperson cannot be discerned. But they pay commissions in excess of ten percent! It's not until some years later that the buyer realizes his mistake, and what he thought he had is not what he has. Invariably, the annuities that pay the highest commission are, of course, the worst for the client.

Most annuities have a flexible commission structure so that the agent can choose how to take her commission. For instance, an all up front commission may be 6%, with no further compensation ever paid. Choice two is usually something like 3% up front, with a .5% trailing commission for perpetuity. The third choice is usually something like 1% up front with a 1% trail. Why would the client "want" his or her agent to get paid as a trail rather than all the commission up front? Simple—to align their interests.

The "trail" as it is called, is like the fee on a fee-only account. It is based on the value of the account, so likewise, the more you make, the more the agent makes, and vice versa. It is this type of structure that gets your advisor wholly on your side, since both of your interests are correlated. Unfortunately, there is no way for clients to know whether their advisors are taking the commission as 100% trail or 100% up front, or something in between.

Oftentimes annuities are sold to you as a tax-deferral instrument, such as an IRA or 401k. But it makes no sense to invest an already tax-deferred account into an annuity for purposes of tax deferral. There may be another valid reason, such as a guaranteed interest rate, or a rider that provides a living benefit, but for tax deferral reasons alone, it provides no additional benefit. In addition, like most other tax-deferred accounts, you could be subject to an early IRS withdrawal penalty of 10% if you withdraw money prior to age 59½. This includes non-qualified, (after-tax) money. Annuities are considered retirement vehicles, so your mindset should be long-term.

Nonetheless, consider very carefully if you are asked to commit to more than nine years. I've never seen any annuity that justifies more than an ten-year surrender schedule. Know what your costs are, which may not be expressed as a fee, but as a cap, participation rate, blended average, spread, et cetera.

If you don't clearly understand what you're getting, and what you're paying, what's guaranteed and what's not, what can be changed by the company and when, then you should not invest. In no event should you let yourself be pressured or rushed to invest in anything—ever. There is no deal so great that it won't be available next week. One week should give you enough time to consider your options, but don't procrastinate; because companies do regularly change their rates, caps, spreads, and other variables.

Note that all benefits are guaranteed by the insurance company, and that no government agency has an express requirement to rescue any policyholders. Of course, we remember what happened with AIG during the Great Recession. Though it may seem unfair at first glance, it is in everyone's interests—particularly the policyholders—that the insurance companies remain solvent and even profitable.

I feel quite confident that the insurance industry can survive almost any financial catastrophe, no matter what currency we may be using. Unlike almost everyone else, insurance companies don't think so much in terms of quarters or years; they think in terms of decades and centuries.

XI

SURVIVING A WORST-CASE SCENARIO

It's hard for most Americans to conceive of a time when a dollar bill has no value. Indeed, I find it very difficult—almost blasphemous—to think of the possibility of life without the American Dollar. But when I look at the hard numbers, coupled with the inconvenient facts of history, I have no logical option, but to conclude that we are on the path of dollar destruction, and the worst-case scenario—no matter how distasteful—could indeed happen. Hope for the best, but plan for the worst, because usually reality is somewhere in between. So, what *is* the worst case?

I think it happens something like this: The Fed continues to raise rates until we slip into another recession. The recession reverberates around the globe. The PIIGS (Portugal, Italy, Ireland, Greece and Spain) get into trouble again. The debt that was only painted over with EU help re-emerges bigger and badder than ever. Old arguments over debt restructuring resurface as the northern economies struggle to sustain the southern ones.

World governments continue to tack on debt as reckless spending, waste and corruption hemorrhage balance sheets. Institutional investors start to see the writing on the wall and begin reducing their exposure. World governments then turn to their central banks to buy their bonds, which, in turn, simply create the money to do so, thus monetizing the debt. Global inflation picks up on a scale not seen since World War II. Riots and protests turn violent worldwide—capitalism is blamed. The masses clamor for an end to capitalism and for some 'savior' to appear.

Enter the International Monetary Fund. They have a currency standing by to replace the dollar and every other currency, called a Special Drawing Right, or SDR, and it is already priced in virtually every currency on the planet.

SDRs per currency unit for January 2018:[42]

Currency	**January 2018**
Chinese Yuan	0.108023
Euro	0.848276
Japanese Yen	0.0063011
U.K. Pound Sterling	0.958455
U.S. Dollar	0.695137
Algerian Dinar	0.00608072
Australian Dollar	0.552981
Bahrain Dinar	1.84877
Botswana Pula	0.0711125
Brazilian Real	0.215794
Brunei Dollar	0.526061
Canadian Dollar	0.559466
Chilean Peso	0.00115531
Colombian Peso	0.000242374
Czech Koruna	0.0333367
Danish Krone	0.11391
Hungarian Forint	0.00275247
Icelandic Krona	0.00675218
Indian Rupee	0.010865
Indonesian Rupiah	5.21757E-05
Iranian Rial	1.90167E-05
Israeli New Sheqel	0.201372
Kazakhstani Tenge	0.00212515

[42]http://www.imf.org/external/np/fin/data/param_rms_mth.aspx

Korean Won	0.000653324
Kuwaiti Dinar	2.31327
Libyan Dinar	0.517491
Malaysian Ringgit	0.17594
Mauritian Rupee	N/A
Mexican Peso	0.0372628
Nepalese Rupee	0.00678447
New Zealand Dollar	0.506338
Norwegian Krone	0.0881605
Rial Omani	1.8079
Pakistani Rupee	0.00628778
Nuevo Sol	0.216554
Philippine Peso	0.0137776
Polish Zloty	0.203799
Qatar Riyal	0.190972
Russian Ruble	0.0122832
Saudi Arabian Riyal	0.18537
Singapore Dollar	0.526061
South African Rand	0.0563704
Sri Lanka Rupee	0.00451618
Swedish Krona	0.0864254
Swiss Franc	0.720947
Thai Baht	0.0217741
Trinidad And Tobago Dollar	0.102857
Tunisian Dinar	0.281597
U.A.E. Dirham	0.189282
Peso Uruguayo	0.0243302
Bolivar Fuerte	0.0696879

The SDR is comprised of the five most utilized currencies. According to the International Monetary Fund, "The respective weights of the U.S. dollar, euro, Chinese renminbi, Japanese yen, and British pound sterling are 41.73 percent, 30.93 percent, 10.92 percent, 8.33 percent, and 8.09 percent. These weights were used to determine the amounts of each of the five currencies included in the new SDR valuation basket that took effect on October 1, 2016."[43]

Currently, the SDR is comprised of these currencies, which is to say that the value of the SDR is being propped up by the value of the underlying currencies. But what if the opposite became true, and the value of the underlying currencies were dependent on the value of the SDR? How would this change things? Since everything is fiat, is it just semantics at this point?

All countries who trade with other countries need a common medium of exchange. Up until the 20th century, that medium was gold and silver. Then it became the U.S. dollar. Today, the SDR is slowly but surely supplanting the U.S. dollar, and loss of the U.S. dollar as the world reserve currency has already begun. The next big move will be a conversion of the petro-dollar to the petro-SDR. This too has already begun.[44]

This is another one of the reasons we hold silver. Gold was confiscated, and could be again.[45] Also, gold is less divisible than silver. There could likely be a period of time when we will convert from dollars to the SDR, and it could be painful. Silver, and junk silver especially, might be candidates for re-emergence as an interim currency.

In other parts of the world, we have seen mass violence and rioting when hyperinflation and other debt crises reached extreme levels. We can see this currently playing out in Venezuela, and in recent years we witnessed it in Argentina.

---

43 IMF. www.imf.org. Special Drawing Right (SDR) October 13, 2017.
44 https://www.itmtrading.com/blog/meet-sdr-new-world-reserve-money/
45 Executive Order 6102, signed on April 5, 1933 by Franklin D. Roosevelt

And though we have always been fortunate to enjoy a more or less stable currency in this country, our days are numbered if we do not get our debt under control. This may sound alarmist, but facts are facts.

Even if our currency is replaced one day, I certainly don't foresee a complete breakdown in society; nor do I see the mass chaos and lingering anarchy that some predict, but there may be a time of transition, and possessing alternative currencies and precious metals could help in the interim.

The point is, though we may believe this could never happen here in the U.S., it has certainly occurred many times and in many places elsewhere in the world. A simple back up plan cannot hurt, and may even prove profitable. It's like my grandfather used to say—a lesson that I never forgot: "It's better to have and not need, than need and not have."

XII

HAS CAPITALISM FAILED US?

One of the saddest developments I have witnessed in my lifetime is the slow yet sure indoctrination that capitalism is inherently evil. Millions of people here in the U.S. and around the world have come out in protest of capitalism, because they see this as the oppressive ideology that has impoverished them. They couldn't be more wrong.

Free market capitalism is the surest way to prosperity—not just for a few, but for the whole.

You can see free market capitalism working on small levels, like local Mom and Pop stores, but on a larger level you have corporations. Some of these corporations are very large, very wealthy, and very powerful. That power extends to the very halls of the U.S. Capitol building.

Perhaps you remember the Occupy Wall Street Movement? While Ex-Goldman guy/U.S. Treasury Secretary Henry Paulson, fellow Ex-Goldman guy/New York Fed President Tim Geithner, and Fed Chairman Ben Bernanke worked diligently to use taxpayer money to bail out Goldman Sachs and some other 1 percenters,[46] the rest of us were dealing with layoffs, foreclosures, and bankruptcies—with no bailouts in sight, just more circular rhetoric and broken promises.

In the midst of all of this emerged a war cry directed against capitalism itself. It is here that I feel some of my fellow 99 percenters may have been misled, believing that what we

[46] http://money.cnn.com/news/specials/storysupplement/bankbailout

actually have is true free market capitalism.

It is not free market capitalism itself that has betrayed us, but rather the cronyism and mercantilism that pervades Washington DC. In a private letter to Col. Mandell House written in 1933, FDR admits that: "The real truth of the matter is, as you and I know, that a financial element in the larger centers has owned the Government ever since the days of Andrew Jackson—and I am not wholly excepting the Administration of W[oodrow] W[ilson]."[47]

In a truly capitalist country, where the government neither favors nor disfavors particular business interests, highly leveraged risk-takers like Goldman Sachs would have failed in 2008 along with Lehman Brothers, to be replaced by more scrupulous and prudent firms. Unfortunately, however, as FDR noted even back in 1933, the powers in DC are beholden to the influence of certain special business interests—special in the sense that they are wealthy, entrenched and organized. And they have a system: the two-party system.

From the very first day in office, the typical politician is thinking about re-election. This costs money—a lot of money. As we have repeatedly witnessed, the politician who spends the most money almost always wins. And so, where do politicians go to get money? To those who have the money, of course—the top 1 percent, through their trusts, corporations, foundations, and Super PACs. And these entities contribute heavily to *both* parties.

So for all *these* individuals, capitalism works perfectly—politicians have power, but need money to get elected and stay elected, and the top 1 percent have money, but need the (use of) politicians' power to further their own (usually corporate) interests.

The obvious problem here is this: You and I aren't getting *any* of the money or *any* of the power. In fact, they're taking *our*

---

[47] President Franklin Delano Roosevelt to Col. Edward Mandell House, November 21, 1933, F.D.R.: His Personal Letters (New York: Duell, Sloan and Pearce 1950), p. 373.

money through taxation and stealing *our* purchasing power through inflation. This is not Capitalism—this is Mercantilism.

As Hernando de Soto observed in his insightful book, *The Other Path*:

> Being a system in which the government of a highly regulated state was *dependent on elite groups which were in turn sustained by state privileges*, mercantilism was vigorously opposed by [...] Adam Smith, the father of economic liberalism. Smith viewed mercantilism as a system in which merchants and industrialists demanded, and the state provided, their own regulations and sources of income.[48]

Sure enough, when Goldman Sachs and friends demanded a bailout, the state provided them one at taxpayer expense—the very raison d'être of the Fed itself. In a truly free market economy, Goldman Sachs would have failed alongside Lehman Brothers and Bear Sterns.

We often hold the naïve assumption that capitalism and other forms of government are mutually exclusive—but this is not so. Indeed, modern day China has taught us that this is incontrovertibly false. China, as the world's second largest economy, with bustling capitalism at almost every level of society, is run by a group of communist families, who themselves profit immensely from this false ideology, thus the need for constant censorship.

At the risk of sounding "un-American", is it not also true that our own socio-economic system is a hybrid somewhat similar to this? But instead of communism at the top, our uniquely American model of economics is a hybrid of capitalism at most levels with mercantilism reigning among the very top echelons.

Surely the baker and the painter and the gardener are all subject to the rules of capitalism, as is the doctor, lawyer and professor. But then again, these are representative of us 99

---

[48] Hernando de Soto, *The Other Path*. 1989. p. 202

percenters. From the perspective of the rest of us, it sure looks like the top 1 percenters get special treatment in much the way de Soto describes, as "a highly regulated state dependent on elite groups which were in turn sustained by state privileges." Perhaps the state itself is not dependent on these elite groups, but our politicians sure are.

So I would say to my fellow 99 percenters: The cycle of money—from these elitists, through their lobbyists, corporations, foundations, and Super-Pacs, to politicians on both sides of the aisle, and then back to the elitists through the state mechanism—is mercantilism, and anathema to free market capitalism.

What's worse, attacks on capitalism itself play right into their hands. A disposal of capitalism means a transition to something else, something worse. A sharing loving world where everyone plays by the rules sounds great on campus, but the outside world just doesn't play that way.

FEEL THE BERN – ALSO KNOWN AS HUNGER

The 2016 presidential election cycle was certainly one to remember. What struck me so dramatically (and with great concern) was the surprising traction Bernie Sanders got as an admitted socialist. Even though I really like him as a person and think his intentions are noble and genuine, he is certainly no free market economist.

Bernie called himself a 'Socialist Democrat.' What is that? Is there really any difference between that and the socialism in Venezuela? You can call Marxism by any name you like, but the end result is always the same. Look at North Korea. What do they call themselves? The Democratic People's Republic of North Korea? There's nothing democratic about it. It looks nothing like a republic, and the poor people are mere slaves, who get shot if they try to leave the country. But they're right on one point—it *is* to the north.

No matter how you cut it, no matter what you call it, when

you take from people who produce and give to those who don't, you are encouraging non-production. This is why 80 million people starved to death in China under Chairman Mao during the "Great Leap Forward." This is why Russia, the largest country in the world—spanning twelve time zones—has an economy no larger than Finland's, more than a century after their "Glorious Revolution." And why Venezuela, with more proven oil reserves than any country on the planet, is forced to import oil. Call it what you want to, the results are always the same: non-production, hunger, and starvation.

If we could jettison the cronyism from our country and truly give free market capitalism a try at the highest levels, used an honest currency and banking system, and maintained a balanced budget, we would see contentment at even the lowest socioeconomic levels. In this type of honest and fair economy, society comes to appreciate fair-mindedness and reacts likewise. Eventually it becomes intuitive; a generation later it becomes intrinsic. Such a society values education as its number one industry, instead of war materiel.

In our current environment of corruption and political favoritism, the average person is beginning to figure out that the system is rigged. For the least fortunate, this realization causes personal resentment and eventually political discord. You can bet we will see many more riots and demonstrations in the years to come as inflation accelerates and the masses clamor for relief from that evil capitalism. "Give us a Socialist!" they will cry.

No, it's not capitalism that has failed us, but we who have failed capitalism.

XIII

YOUR EXECUTIVE SUMMARY

So much for the ideological; let's get back to the empirical. The point of this guide is to protect our portfolios, and protect our livelihood. I've pointed out a lot of things that may be new to you, and some things no doubt seem controversial and maybe even unsavory. My sole intention here is to show you the factors that we consider when managing our portfolios, but as I've said before, every investor is different, every situation is different. And of course, just because a certain strategy has worked well in the past does not guarantee that it will in the future. Nonetheless, if you feel that some of what I've said here resonates with you, you may want to consider working with a Certified Financial Planner to better evaluate how these principals may be applied to your personal situation.

So, let's review what we've learned thus far:

- The market is driven by investors. Investors are people. People are emotional about their money and often make irrational decisions.
- The things that we thought moved the market are not what really moves the market.
- The boom and bust cycle is created by the expansion and subsequent contraction of the money supply. The Federal Reserve is responsible for this activity.
- The Fed drops interest rates after a crash. This is called stimulus. Monetary expansion ensues. Markets don't crash during expansionary periods, they boom.

- The markets only crash when the money supply is contracting, i.e., when interest rates are rising, and/or the Fed is reducing the balance sheet. This is now occurring.
- The interest rate that was required to crash the market in 2000 was 6.5%. In 2008, it was 5.25%. We worry that the next crash would occur at a rate lower than 5.25%. Of course, no one can predict the *actual* rate.
- Once the Fed Funds Rate hits 2.75%, for every quarter point hike thereafter, we are moving 10% out of riskier assets.
- Assets come in all shapes and sizes, and these rotate in and out of favor over time. There is no perfect asset class for all markets. Thus, we must diversify.
- We are diversifying into a safety basket of 1-3 year treasuries, 3-5 year treasuries, and 5-7 year treasuries. We use very inexpensive index funds or ETFs.
- We are starting with the shorter terms first and going longer as interest rates move above 4%.
- Another option may be to look at an annuity to guarantee part of our portfolio.
- We are diversifying some of our dollars (less than 10%) into precious metals, particularly silver.
- Do not abandon asset allocation and diversification.
- When buying silver, we are buying only U.S. Silver Eagles and "junk silver", which is pre-1965 quarters, dimes, and half-dollars.
- We're also keeping some cash on hand. About $10,000 in hundreds, twenties, and tens.
- Do not store any of this at the bank or any other regulated institution. Can you get to it on Christmas morning at 4 am? If not, move it.
- Obviously, once the crash has occurred, we would want to reverse the process, selling off our longer-term bonds first, and buying into the asset classes that have

suffered the most dramatic sell offs. Usually, this is emerging markets.

Finally, we must always expect the unexpected. As Donald Rumsfeld put it, "There's what we know we know, and there's what we know we don't know. But there's also what we don't know we don't know," and against this we must always be vigilant. Diversification and redundancy, preparation and planning; these will serve you well.

Again, I want to reiterate that nothing herein should be taken as specific investment advice. I have no idea about your current holdings, your risk tolerance, your future goals, your wants or needs, or anything else. All I am doing here is telling you what we are doing, and have done, for our clients in general. I am giving you my rationale for why we have taken and plan to take these actions, but you have to decide what is right for you.

Nonetheless, through considering our actions and taking heed of the short lessons here, you should be better armed to face the coming onslaught of the next major market correction. Hopefully, it won't be as bad as 2008, since the mortgage industry doesn't look like it did back then, and the banks are flush with cash. But there are plenty of other issues out there, and it will be interesting to see which of them bring about a correction. Others will say a correction is not going to result, that the Fed will stop raising rates at the right time, but history does not support that assumption.

Indeed, history is replete with exhilarating booms only to be followed by devastating busts. Create your action plan now and see it through. It will be difficult to sell out of the market and pile up in treasuries when the market continues to scream, and it will be difficult to buy back in once the market has dropped 40%. You will ask yourself, "what if it goes to zero? I will lose everything." Just remember the one phrase that will always confound your best-laid plans: "This time it's different."

BIBLIOGRAPHY

Cochran, John and Fred Glahe. *The Hayek-Keynes Debate-Lessons for Current Business Cycle Research.* New York: The Edwin Mellen Press. 1999.

De Soto, Hernando. *The Other Path: The Economic Answer to Terrorism.* New York: Harper & Row. 1989.

Ekelund, Robert Jr., and Robert Hebert. *A History of Economic Theory and Method.* Long Grove: Waveland Press. 2007.

Ferguson, Niall. *The Ascent of Money: A Financial History of the World.* New York: Penguin Press. 2008.

Fergusson, Adam. *When Money Dies: The Nightmare Deficit Spending, Devaluation, and Hyperinflations in Weimar Germany.* New York: Public Affairs. 2010.

Griffin, G. Edward. *The Creature from Jekyll Island: A Second Look at the Federal Reserve.* Westlake Village: American Media. 1994.

Hayek, F.A. *The Fatal Conceit: The Errors of Socialism.* Chicago: The University of Chicago Press. 1988.

Hayek, F.A. *The Road to Serfdom.* Chicago: The University of Chicago Press. 2007.

Hazlitt, Henry. *Economics in One Lesson.* New York: Three Rivers Press. 1979.

Keynes, John Maynard. *The General Theory of Employment, Interest and Money.* New York: Classic Books America. 2009.

Lebor, Adam. *The Tower of Basel: The Shadowy History of the Secret Bank That Runs the World.* New York: Public Affairs. 2013.

Mandelbrot, Benoit and Richard Hudson. *The Misbehavior of Markets: A Fractal View of Financial Turbulence.* New York: Basic Books. 2004.

Mises, Ludwig Von. *The Theory of Money and Credit.* Lexington: Pacific Publishing Studio. 2010.

Mises, Ludwig Von. *The Human Action: A Treatise on Economics.* Auburn: Ludwig Von Mises Institute. 1998.

Paul, Ron. *End the Fed.* New York: Grand Central Publishing. 2009.

Paulson, Henry Jr. *On the Brink: Inside the Race to Stop the Collapse of the Global Financial System.* New York: Business Plus. 2010.

Rickards, James. *The Death of Money: The Coming Collapse of the International Monetary System.* New York: Penguin Group. 2014.

Rothbard, Murray. *The Case against the Fed.* Auburn: Ludwig von Mises Institute. 2007.

Senholz, Hans. *The Age of Inflation.* Belmont: Western Islands. 1979.

Steil, Benn. *The Battle of Bretton Woods.* New Jersey: Princeton University Press. 2013.

ABOUT J. KEVIN MEADERS

J. Kevin Meaders founded Magellan Planning Group in 2003 to address the lack of coordination among and between the three major disciplines: Legal, Financial, and Tax. He realized that rarely, if ever, do clients' advisors meet or even communicate directly on behalf of their client. There was a clear need for tri-disciplinary, coordinated planning. He brought financial planning, tax planning and estate planning together under one roof to maximize coordination among the disciplines for the benefit of his clients and their families.

Kevin has given countless financial and estate planning seminars since his career began in 1994, in northern Metro Atlanta. He has been published in both local and national publications and is a regular speaker for both individuals and professional organizations. Kevin has hosted "The Magellan Planning Hour" radio show and taught at Emory University's Evenings at Emory. He also is a regular instructor for the Georgia Society of CPAs.

Kevin graduated from Oglethorpe University in Atlanta with a double B.A. in Philosophy and Political Science. He earned a Juris Doctor degree (J.D.) from Georgia State University College of Law with a focus on estate planning and trust law. Additionally, he has earned the designations of CERTIFIED FINANCIAL PLANNER™ (CFP®), Chartered Financial Consultant (ChFC) and Chartered Life Underwriter (CLU).

Kevin's favorite professional activity is designing and creating charitable trusts, which allow a taxpayer to dispose of highly appreciated property without the associated tax burdens. Kevin helps citizens minimize their taxes, maximize their dependable income, and give back to their community and the things that mean the most to them.

An Atlanta native, Kevin's family settled in Georgia in the late 1780's and is widely known for Meaders Pottery, which has some pieces proudly displayed in the Smithsonian. Kevin still calls Atlanta home and lives with his family in the Brookhaven area.

Made in the USA
Coppell, TX
05 November 2026

11315628R00057